make your own
digital photo
scrapbook

make your own
digital photo
scrapbook

Roger Pring and Ivan Hissey

ILEX

First published in the United Kingdom in 2005 by

I L E X

The Old Candlemakers
West Street
Lewes
East Sussex BN7 2NZ
www.ilex-press.com

This book was conceived by
ILEX, Cambridge, England

Publisher: Alastair Campbell
Executive Publisher: Sophie Collins
Creative Director: Peter Bridgewater
Managing Editor: Tom Mugridge
Editor: Kylie Johnston
Design Manager: Tony Seddon
Designer: Alistair Plumb
Junior Designer: Jane Waterhouse

Illustrator and Photographer: Ivan Hissey
Contributors: Roger Pring, Peter Cope, Chris Middleton

British Library Cataloguing-in-Publication Data
A catalogue record for this book is available from the British Library

ISBN 1-904705-62-6

Printed and bound in China

For more information on this title please visit:
www.web-linked.com/dpscuk

Contents

It's time to throw away the scissors and glue

Scrapbooks used to be about scissors, paper, and glue. But today digital technology can be used to bring your family photos and memorabilia – your memories, in fact – to life in ways that were unimaginable just a few years ago. So if you've got a computer and an Internet connection (even if it's just your normal phone line) plus a bit of imagination, then you can transform your ancestors' photos, your holiday souvenirs, your videos of family and friends, even children's drawings and snapshots of pets, into an interactive experience that you can publish online, put onto CD, or email your friends – wherever in the world they might be!

You don't need to have all the latest equipment; just a computer (it doesn't matter if it's a PC or a Mac), a printer – and that Internet connection.

You'll also need to have some way of getting your snaps onto your computer. If you have a digital still or video camera, then that's ideal; if not, you'll need a scanner.

A CD writer (either built into your computer or external) would help, but there are ways around this if you don't have one yet. But remember: all this kind of equipment is getting cheaper by the day, so the investment might not be as large as you think!

So let's get started. By the end of this book you'll have mastered the techniques, not just of preserving your favourite mementoes and immortalizing those special memories, but also of giving them a new lease of life. The Internet is truly a global network, and it's growing by the second: why not be part of it and share your passions and memories with the people you care about the most, wherever they happen to be? And maybe you could make new contacts and friends in the process... they're all out there at the click of a mouse. We'll show you how to do all this and much, much more. But first, here's the science part... then it's on to the projects. Got your ideas ready? Let's go!

All you need to know about...

This book is all about the fun projects you can do with a bit of imagination, a computer, a camera, and some other useful pieces of digital technology. But you may be thinking, 'I don't know anything about computers, or the Internet!' Well, we've got news for you: neither do most people; they just like what digital technology can do for them. And you will too, if you follow the projects. But first, here's a quick run-through of what the technology is, and what it does...

Inside your computer

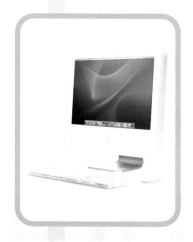

Always at the cutting edge of hardware and operating system design, Apple's iMac has quickly become a design icon. More importantly for you, it has some great built-in image-handling talents. In fact, like most Apple products, its favourite job is handling digital images. With a powerful G5 processor, you'll soon be flying!

If you already know your way around the inside of your computer, skip this introduction. But if you want to find out more about it and some of the other gadgets you might have invested in to go with it, then read on. It will help you get the most out of the projects later in the book.

The chances are that your computer, if it's a fairly recent design, already has the built-in capabilities for most of the creative stuff we've got lined up for you. And when you need to add new items, like extra memory or a scanner, we'll show you how – and what they're capable of!

Getting the information in

So, how do you get the pictures in? There are three main methods. The first option is to connect a digital camera directly to an input socket on the computer, or take the storage card from the camera and slot it into a card reader (which is in turn connected to the computer). If you don't have any of these, don't worry. Many perfectly good digital cameras are comparatively cheap nowadays, and prices are falling all the time as the technology improves.

But if you don't want to make the investment, there are other options, such as using a scanner. Any picture or document – or even a small object that can be placed (carefully!) on the scanner glass – is easily captured and fed directly into your computer.

If you don't have a scanner (you'll find they're fairly inexpensive) you could always use your computer's built-in CD drive to input images from a PhotoCD, as well as from commercial clip-art and photo collections.

With today's computers and the Internet, there's literally a whole world of possibilities out there for creative minds. And unlike a paper-based scrapbook or photo album, you'll find all your pictures, text, and memorabilia can be almost infinitely changed, updated – and preserved in time.

Beyond this, why not use your email connection to swap your own pictures with friends and family? There are also millions of copyright-free pictures you could download from the Internet (but make sure they really are copyright-free before distributing them to your friends!).

As technology prices drop, even a computer as small and portable as this Apple iBook has the speed, memory, and processing power to handle digital images with ease.

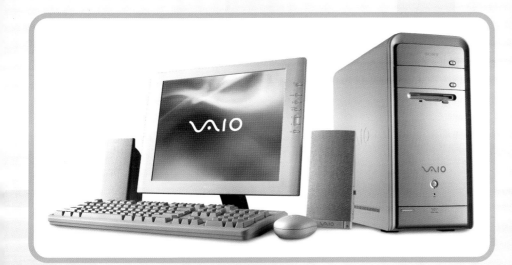

By far the most common hardware and software platform, the Windows PC has grabbed the world's attention over the last decade. Because it's so common – well over three-quarters of the world's wired population has one – you can be sure nearly all the software and hardware you buy will be compatible with it. This Sony Vaio RS model (also available in laptop versions) is designed for the kind of work we'll be doing. A DVD burner comes as standard for sharing large files.

Storage and memory

Computers are highly organized machines, and you'll need to be ultra-organized when it comes to picture filing, so that all the projects you embark on work quickly and easily. But where does all the information get stored? While they're being worked on, your pictures are held temporarily in what's called RAM (random access memory). When the job's done, it's stored on your hard drive (actually a stack of magnetic disks inside your computer's case).

The capacity of both memory and storage is measured in megabytes, and this is one of the specifications you'll see used to compare one computer with another. Luckily, recent technology has come to the rescue of those of us who need to handle large files like digital images. A new computer will typically have 256 or 512 megabytes (MB) of RAM, and its hard drive may have 60,000 to 200,000 megabytes of storage space – handily described as 60 to 200 gigabytes (GB).

You'll come across lots of terms and abbreviations like these once you start using your computer and the Internet regularly. But why is all this important? Well, the point to remember is that more RAM lets you work with more powerful software and larger files – such as high-quality pictures and video – while more storage lets you keep more of the resulting work on your hard drive. To store even more files, and pass them on to other computer users, you may also want to invest in peripheral storage devices (see page 22).

The processor

Otherwise known as the CPU, the central processing unit is where all the calculating power of the computer is concentrated. It doesn't matter whether the computer is working out your tax return, improving your Christmas photographs, or building a web page, the same chips are processing information at break-neck speed. The CPU's 'clock speed' is expressed in megahertz (MHz) and gigahertz, and there is a continuous scramble among manufacturers for the highest rating. Apple's Macintosh computers use slightly different chips, which generally give similar performance with a lower clock speed.

The screen

The conventional computer monitor is much like your TV screen, although capable of showing much higher resolution. Three 'guns' at the back of its 'cathode-ray tube' (CRT) fire precise patterns of electrons at red, green and blue phosphors on the inside of the screen. Bulky CRT monitors are increasingly being replaced by LCD (liquid crystal display) screens, which are more expensive but much neater.

Getting the information out

Colour inkjet printers now provide quality indistinguishable from an original photo. The final picture appearance is dependent on the resolution of your images (see page 15), but you can also balance ink and paper costs against quality.

All about software

Your computer arrived with its own basic program built in. This 'operating system' (OS) software takes care of all the fundamental tasks like starting up the computer, managing files, connecting to add-on ('peripheral') hardware like printers, scanners, and digital cameras – and finally putting the system to sleep at the end of a session. It runs quietly in the background and, with luck on your side, you need never notice it. More recent machines have smarter and more stable operating systems, but they all do the same basic job.

Beyond the basics

To do any useful work, you need more software. As a minimum, you need to be able to organize, size, trim, and enhance your pictures. The choice of software is vast and growing almost daily. If you want to change the colour of the paint on the front door in that old photo from the 1970s, insert an absent family member into an existing group photo, reduce the effect of those telltale wrinkles, or wrap your holiday pictures around an animated globe, there are programs competing for your money. And each software package encourages you to follow the inevitable, and costly, upgrade path.

Take a moment to reflect on your choice. Maybe start with a basic 'image-editing' program. Something like Adobe Photoshop Elements 3 (available for both Windows and Apple Mac machines) gives you the power to do basic photo retouching and correcting (including removal of the inevitable 'red eye'), merge one picture with another, create a complete photo story, and finally produce prints, emails, or web pages. This program is available in a try-out version (you get 30 days of free use) as a download from the Adobe website, *www.adobe.com*. See page 18 to check out the whole business of Internet connection. If you don't have a fast Internet connection, persuade a friend to download it for you – it's a lot of megabytes, but won't take too long to download on a cable or broadband connection. If any of these terms seems mysterious, see page 152 for a detailed explanation.

What about the words?

You'll have a simple text editing or 'word processing' program on your machine – Windows PCs and Macs each have their own as standard – but it may limit your freedom of choice in terms of layout and design. At the other end of the scale, full-size word processing programs such as Microsoft Word (often available at a discount when you buy your computer) offer greater control over every aspect of type handling, and you can easily import your pictures so they sit right in the page alongside the words. You may find that the number of functions available is overwhelming. There's usually an escape hatch provided in the form of a set of templates where many of the necessary decisions have been taken already, leaving you to feed your material into predetermined slots. See page 28 for a typical project using a word processing program like this. You'll also find your computer has a range of different typefaces (lettering styles, or 'fonts') supplied with its operating system.

They'll vary from the plain and utilitarian to the more exotic, and it's easy to add lots more – there are thousands available on the Internet and on the cover-mounted CDs of computer and digital photography magazines. So go and browse!

A step further

When you've got a sizeable collection of pictures, you might consider getting a database program, both to organize and display your work. Look at the website of a huge commercial photographic agency (try *www.imageexpress.com*) to see how they employ this type of software to help customers to search for pictures by 'keywords', and eventually purchase images online. But let's take this one step at a time. An ordinary spreadsheet program can be surprisingly useful in displaying your images. We suggest some ideas on page 48 for creating an eye-catching, interactive calendar.

Digital cameras

If you're a photo buff, you'll already have information overload about the competing qualities of dozens of digital cameras. You may even have distilled this information enough to make a choice and part with your money. In which case, you'll know that however many millions of pixels of resolution there are in your new camera, it's not as many as the new models that have already appeared at lower prices. If you're not a photo buff, you still need to have an idea what all this means, since resolution, pixels, and the rest are vital concepts in understanding how pictures arrive on

paper or on the screen. Even if you don't plan to shoot digital pictures, you'll still need a grasp of the terms when it comes to manipulating your photos and getting them into shape for presentation. There's no way around it!

Do more dots mean better pictures?

In a normal film camera, light falls onto sensitive film. The processed image consists of millions of tiny, coloured grains – so many, in fact, that the brain is fooled into thinking that the eyes see a continuous, smooth blend of colour. In a digital camera, the film is replaced by a type of computer chip which is sensitive to light. The millions of film grains are replaced by

Left: Canon's EOS-1Ds Mark II digital camera captures more than 16 million pixels in a shot – enough to impress even the most ardent film aficionado. Then again, it does cost an arm and a leg.

Above: Consumer models such as the Digital Ixus 40 are much more affordable. As well as a useful 4 megapixels, this one has 3x optical zoom, so with a press of a button the action is three times closer.

Because pictures destined for TV screens need lower resolutions than photos, good-quality MiniDV digital video cameras such as this one from Sony cost little more than digital still cameras. If your computer has a FireWire socket, you can plug the camera straight in.

millions of tiny 'cells', each one a receptor for red, green, or blue wavelengths of light. Each of these millions of receptors records the amount of light striking it. The information from all of them is gathered into a single, computer-readable file and stored temporarily in the camera.

So far, so straightforward, but are the pictures any good? Surely these receptors can't be as tiny and detailed as the grains in photographic film? Well, firstly, they're getting pretty close nowadays, and secondly, it all depends what you want your pictures for. Colour film can be used to make a 20 x 16 inch print with little or no perceptible grain structure to spoil the effect. Most digital cameras still have some way to go to match that level, but many affordable ones have four or five million pixels ('megapixels'), enough for at least a 10 x 8 inch print of similar quality. This is easily sufficient for everyday album use, and more than you could ever need for a website.

Large image files need lots of storage, both in the camera's memory card and on your computer. So, be prepared to see your hard disk invaded by very large quantities of data – but we'll show you how to avoid being buried alive! On the plus side, digital photography means point, shoot, download – there's no wait, and no charge for processing.

The maths of image resolution

Your computer screen (displaying about 96 pixels across and down each inch, quoted as 'points per inch') shows at least 1024 pixels across the screen by 768 down: that's over three-quarters of a million pixels. But put your nose up to the monitor and you can see the dots. Although it looks bright and clear, it would make a poor-quality print. Now imagine a typical camera with a 4 megapixel capability. It can make a picture around 2200 pixels across by 1800 down. This would cover your screen four times over – or, more usefully in

practice, could be squeezed down to produce a postcard-size print with dots too small to detect with the naked eye.

As you output a digital image at a smaller size, the resolution increases. Output resolution is usually quoted in dots per inch ('dpi'), and in practice you need about 300 dpi to fool the eye. So you need more pixels in an image to print it at 300 dpi than you do to display it on-screen, at the same size, at 96 ppi. (You can look up all these terms in our *Glossary*.) 'Headache' is what you get trying to understand all this, but smugness is what you feel when you get the point!

Digital cameras eat batteries for breakfast, lunch and dinner – especially if you use the built-in LCD screen. Most can take ordinary 'AA' batteries, but it's wise to invest in a rechargeable pack, charged using a 'docking cradle' such as this one from Fuji. You can also keep the cradle connected to your computer, and connect the camera just by dropping it in.

Scanners

Digital photography is a relatively new activity. Film- or plate-based photography dates from the middle of the nineteenth century, back when people got a reputation for being stiff and unemotional because they had to stay still for the camera. So if you're lucky enough to have ancestors with a sense of history, you may possess pictures from over 150 years ago. Even for the majority of us not so blessed, there's still an extraordinary treasure trove of photographs, movies, objects, newspaper clippings, diaries, letters, postcards, certificates and diplomas, drawings, legal documents, books, and other evocative items waiting to be reborn. If you have no such history, concentrate on the present – and start one!

The hp ScanJet 4670 is a unique type of scanner that's completely see-through. Rather than laying your documents on top of one glass plate, you sandwich them between two. You can also scan large objects by placing the scanner on top, or even scan from the side. That's what we call versatile!

Acquiring the image

To get all these 'legacy' images into usable form you need a scanner. Relentless competition among manufacturers has made a basic scanner less expensive than a reasonable meal for two. If you've just bought a computer, your supplier may well have bundled the scanner in for 'free', and most scanners come with their own basic software.

Most of these simple scanners are 'flatbed' designs, intended to deal with ordinary letter-size originals and smaller items. You lift the lid, place the image face-down on the glass plate, and set the relevant software going. Usually the scanning function will form part of an image-editing program. After the scanning lamp has passed quickly across the image area, your screen will show a preview window offering a low-resolution scan of the subject and the opportunity to set a number of controls (see *opposite* for a practical example). You might decide to scan part of the image, and 'crop out' the rest.

The machine is set up to expose for the 'average' original. Change the settings if necessary, hit *OK* and a slower pass will

Never the Twain shall meet? Nonsense! Almost every scanner comes with 'Twain' software that hooks into your computer's operating system. Image-editing programs such as Photoshop Elements understand Twain, so regardless of which scanner you're using they can give you the option of kick-starting it from the *Import* menu. In this way, you can scan images directly into your editing software... then it's over to you!

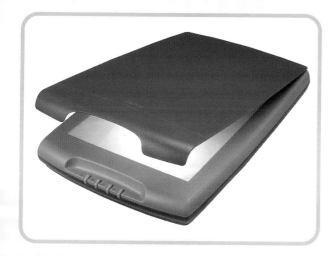

This handsome Umax scanner is typical of the flatbed type that you can buy separately at relatively low cost, or, with some makes, get bundled with new PCs. They come with their own software, or you can buy a more sophisticated scanning package if you wish, but it's almost certainly unnecessary. In any event, most scanning software operates in a similar way (see *below*). Simply place your original on the glass, close the lid, and fire.

Your scanner will come with its own software (Epson's is shown *below*) to control the scanning process. Part of its job is to adjust the colour and tone of the scan to give you a result that's strong and clear while remaining as faithful as possible to the photo you're scanning. Although you have the option of fiddling with colour and tone controls manually, you can usually leave all this in the safe hands of the software – all you have to do is tell it what resolution you need and let it get on with the job. If you'd rather have even more control, and maybe advanced features like 'batch scanning' to deal with large numbers of pictures, you could buy a separate scanning program such as VueScan (*bottom*), available from *www.hamrick.com*.

produce an image at your chosen size and resolution. Many scanners come with a 'transparency hood', a lid that contains extra hardware to acquire images by projecting light through a slide or transparency. The main difference is the greatly increased scanning resolution required to get a useable result from a 35mm original, for example. Dust and debris become, literally, a bigger problem, so a can of compressed air is handy to clean your slides first. The 'optics' – lenses and mirrors inside the scanner – also become much more critical, and the average flatbed will turn in rather fuzzy results.

If you have a lot of transparencies to deal with, consider purchasing a dedicated film scanner. Results from these more costly machines are usually much better, especially in capturing the dynamic range of transparency film – but if you are determined never to shoot transparency film again, rent or borrow one for a while and patiently scan the cream of your collection for future use.

Size and resolution

Even a simple flatbed scanner will offer a huge ratio of enlargement (or reduction). The initial temptation to scan everything at high resolution (say 600 dots per inch) and at 300% enlargement will soon subside at the sight of the resulting file sizes filling up your computer. And there is no point scanning an old, out-of-focus photo at high resolution; all you'll get is a big, soft mess. Try instead to predict the eventual size you'll need, then set the controls accordingly.

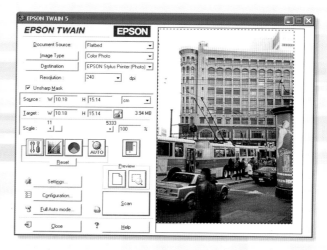

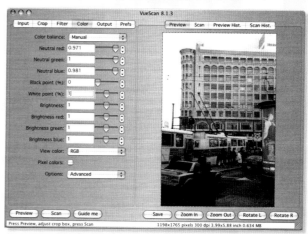

The Internet

SOFTWARE

DIGITAL CAMERAS

SCANNERS

▶ THE INTERNET

PRINTERS

DIGITAL MEDIA

The best parts of the Internet comprise a marvellous resource for inspiration in designing and organizing your photo scrapbook. The worst might turn your hair grey, if it isn't already. You can look at everything from tin toy collecting sites, online auction services, and archives of rare postcards, to websites created at enormous cost by corporations selling everything from tequila to toothbrushes. Look, admire, and, most of all, borrow their ideas. Alternatively, feel much better about your own creative abilities once you've laughed at the competition.

Getting connected

Skip this if you're already online. The simplest kind of connection, and the slowest, is 'dial-up', which works via your existing phone line. You'll need a modem (standard with most computers, but also available to add on) and the phone

number of an 'ISP' (Internet service provider). Your computer may already contain details for one or more ISPs, and 'browser' software to navigate the 'world wide web' – the pages of words and pictures you'll access via the Internet. Rather than setting up the connection manually, you can use a software CD provided by an ISP – you'll often find them given away with computer magazines. This will contain all you need to connect to that particular provider. You should be able to choose whether to pay a monthly fee for unlimited access (sometimes with certain restrictions), which means you pay the ISP but the phone connection is free, or 'pay as you go', where you just clock up a few pence per minute on your phone bill whenever you're connected. See our *Glossary* for more on the technical terms that 'cyberspace' is rife with.

For much faster access, you can get a 'broadband' connection either by converting your phone line ('ADSL') or by having a new digital cable installed, along with a cable TV service if you want it. You'll usually have to sign up for a year, and either pay an installation fee or buy your own digital modem. Monthly fees are pricier than for dial-up, but well worth it if you use the Internet more than occasionally. With broadband, you're connected 24 hours a day, and you don't have to 'log off' before you can use the phone.

What's it for?

The Internet is the world's biggest library, so how do you find all the stuff on its virtual shelves? Well, the Net is patrolled by 'bots'. Yes, that's short for 'robots' – but not the tin men of

Google (*www.google.com*) is one of the best search engines – you can use it to find pictures, too, and opt to filter out results containing 'adult' content.

We've done a picture search and a general search for *"family tree"*. Google turned up 7,500 images in less than a quarter of a second, and more than 750,000 related websites in a quarter of that time! If you refined the search using your own family name, you might dig up some ancestors…

science fiction. These pieces of intelligent software search the entire interconnected network for documents and websites, constantly incorporating new material as it comes online.

There are dozens of specialist 'search engine' websites, each powered by their own teams of bots. Think of them as your intelligent and endlessly patient librarians. In reality, a search engine is a powerful array of computers that stores and organizes billions of references. Rather than sifting through the whole Internet – billions of pages of information – you can search this database for matching references. It's surprisingly fast, and often a search engine will even find documents that actually match what you're looking for.

Try calling up a search engine, such as Google at *www.google.com*, and enter a single chosen word. Let's say you were looking for references to *yorkshire* (capital letters are ignored). Google will respond in well under a second with more than six million web page references (or 'hits', to use the jargon). If you search for the same term in a year's time, that figure will probably be much higher, as more and more

sites are added to the Internet. Obviously it pays to be more specific! Try again with *'south yorkshire'* (use quotation marks to look for a whole phrase) and you get just over a million hits – better, but still far too much reading. Try *'south yorkshire' +ancestors* (the plus sign means you only want pages that include this word too) and you're down to about 2,500. Inserting a family name gets you nearly down to the wire: *'south yorkshire' +ancestors +roberts* produces only 200 results.

As well as letting you admire people's websites, the Internet plugs you into a worldwide community of special-interest groups. If you need help in constructing a family tree, there's a legion of people who know all about genealogy; when you're struggling to restore an old photograph on-screen, you'll find tutorial pages from the software developer or from experts and enthusiasts; if you'd like to see what the newspapers said on the day your mother was born, there's a good chance that an old archive will have extracts.

Search engines will dig up millions of online communities of hobbyists, collectors, writers, photographers… and somewhere among these you should be able to find what you're looking for. By joining one or many of these communities, you'll quickly find yourself part of a global network of people who share your passions and enthusiasms – and quite a few who don't!

Printers

SOFTWARE

DIGITAL CAMERAS

SCANNERS

THE INTERNET

▶ **PRINTERS**

DIGITAL MEDIA

When the time comes to print out your picture, the aim is to preserve all the quality that was recorded by the camera or scanner – perhaps with your contribution of retouching and adjustment. The computer monitor shows a bright, saturated image, and it may take a while to accept that no printer is ever going to reproduce that brilliance. Your monitor emits light, but printed paper can only reflect it. While the monitor combines red, green, and blue light to make up any colour that's needed, your picture file is reproduced by the printer as microscopic dots of cyan (light blue), magenta (a vivid pink), yellow, and black ink – 'CMYK' for short. The page you're reading now was produced on a printing press, but it's similar to an inkjet printout in that it contains up to 2,500 CMYK dots across and down every inch.

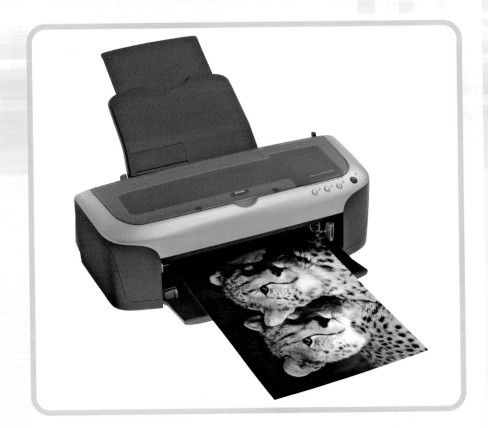

One of the by-products of digital technology becoming smaller, faster, and less expensive with each new generation has been that computers and their peripheral devices, like printers, have become simpler and more attractive to look at. In the wake of Apple's iMac, PC hardware has jumped on the design bandwagon. This Epson inkjet printer is sleek and compact, yet can turn out photo-quality prints at A3 size – if your images are up to it.

Colour printing technology ranges from the quiet desktop inkjet, like this neat and low-cost Epson (*right*), to larger professional devices that can turn out poster-sized originals, like this hp DesignJet (*below*). But stick with the former... unless your ambition gets the better of you.

Going dotty for pixels?

These physical dots of ink are not the same as pixels. That's why professionals try to avoid talking about *image* resolution in 'dots per inch' (dpi), when they really mean pixels per inch (ppi) – because it's all too easy to confuse this with *printing* resolution. But 'dpi' just seems to have caught on as an all-purpose measure of resolution, so you always need to keep in mind which sort of dots you're dealing with.

Remember, the printer only has those four colours of ink (a few use six), but your digital images can contain more than 16 million different colours. To reproduce them all, the printer has to use a whole lot of tiny dots to make up a single pixel. Luckily you don't have to work out how many pixels per inch to use, because somebody else already has, and it turns out that about 150 is ideal. In practice, though, the pixels in the image might not line up exactly with the printer's clusters of dots. The solution is to double the resolution to 300. So that's why images destined for printing are normally stored at 300 dpi. But, as you'll have gathered, this is all just a rough guide – it won't make any difference if you scale an image up or down a bit and end up with, say, 265 or 346 pixels per inch.

Print and paper

Exactly how does the printer translate on-screen colours into print? That's up to its 'driver' software. Each printer maker has its own method of enhancing colour, but you can turn this off and make manual adjustments if you don't approve.

Inkjet printers demand special papers. Although you can use ordinary photocopier paper – there's normally a setting to reduce ink flow for this – you won't get photo-quality output on it. There are high-gloss coated papers, silk and matt finish, heavyweight card, decal papers for decorating sweatshirts and ceramics, CD labels, long rolls for banners and panoramas, and even canvas-textured paper. You can also buy 'archive' papers and inks guaranteed to preserve your precious pictures for decades to come.

Speaking of ink... Inkjet printers are cheap these days, but ink isn't. Black will run out first, and is replaced separately. Some models have separate tanks for each colour, so you don't have to throw away a cartridge before they're all finished. But running costs are always an important concern.

Saving to digital media

SOFTWARE

DIGITAL CAMERAS

SCANNERS

THE INTERNET

PRINTERS

▶ DIGITAL MEDIA

We've already looked at saving pictures on your own hard disk, but there are two other crucial storage issues: backing up data and moving it between locations. First, and most important, is the need to store a backup copy of your vital files. Imagine this sequence of events: you fill up the camera's storage with lots of pictures. You transfer them to your computer, work on them, and integrate them into an album or project. Then you have second thoughts and start to make different adjustments to copies of your shots. After a while you have several copies of each photo, in total representing an irreplaceable set of pictures and a lot of hard work. And it's all on the same magnetic disks spinning away inside your computer. Only when your hard disk has expired without hope of recovery, or someone has walked away with your laptop, will you become a true believer in backup.

Media types

The floppy disk is all but dead, since it doesn't hold enough information to be any use. Realistic solutions start with CD-R (recordable compact disc), and recent computers allow you to record a CD right in the slot where you normally read them. If yours doesn't, you can buy an external CD writer.

A standard CD-R holds up to 700MB – room for 100 A4-size pictures saved as JPEG files (see page 44 for more on file formats). CD-Rs are cheap and reliable, and easy to store and catalogue. You can also use just part of a disc, and fill the rest up at another 'session'. Writing is fairly slow (and will occasionally fail), and CD-Rs can't be erased and reused. CD-RW (rewriteable) overcomes that objection, but this type of disc is more likely to degrade and lose your data over time.

DVD (digital video – or 'versatile' – disc) is increasingly common, and gives you much more storage space. The DVD-R format can store movies from your computer that will play

Far left: Zip disks, holding up to 750MB, are probably the most popular form of removable storage. You need the right Zip drive for the type of disk. Newer formats such as REV store a lot more data in slightly larger cartridges.
Left: Keyring-sized 'flash memory' devices plug into your computer's USB socket for instant access.
Right: Compact Flash cards slot into your digital camera.
Below: IBM's Microdrive looks like a memory card, but in fact contains a miniaturized hard disk.

back on a standard DVD player connected to your TV (more about this on page 90). More useful for general storage are the two rival rewriteable formats, DVD-RW and DVD+RW (did you spot the difference?), each with a capacity of 4.7GB. New double-layer DVD-R DL drives can store up to 8.5GB.

As an alternative to these 'optical' formats, 'removable drives' take hard-disk-like technology and split it between a drive and a cartridge. So you have a drive installed in or attached to your computer, and any number of cartridges that you can slot in and out, write and rewrite as you please. Iomega is the leading company here. Its Zip disks come in 100, 250, and 750MB sizes, and the REV drive takes 35GB cartridges that cost only about £1 per gigabyte.

The final storage option is an external hard disk, which, using interfaces such as FireWire, you can plug in and unplug without fuss, yet can hold at least as much and work at least as fast as the main one built into your computer.

Far left: Hang on, that's a music player, not a storage device! True, but Apple's iPod contains a large hard drive, and can be used to store your image files as well as digital music tracks – though it can't show you your holiday snaps while you're on the bus (yet).
Left: Iomega's REV system stores an amazing 35GB in each handy cartridge. The drive is pricey, but cartridges are surprisingly affordable.
Right: Although CD and DVD are well established as the two basic optical storage media, each has a number of variants. DVD is particularly annoying, with two rewriteable options and dual-layer to contend with. LaCie's d2 DVD±RW drive represents one of the very few ways to read and write all the current formats in just one box. And, designed by FA Porsche, it'll look great on your desktop while it does so.

Your home page

Despite the vast and ever-increasing extent of the Internet, there are millions of megabytes of unused webspace whirling around on web servers worldwide. Almost everyone who ever signed up for an Internet connection received, as part of the deal, a patch of virgin territory (usually around 20MB of webspace). This might sound meagre given the huge amounts of file storage discussed on earlier pages, but it's more than enough of a plot on which to cultivate a flourishing home page. Wagonloads of visitors are sure to pass by, appreciating your fine crops of images and finely wrought text.

Looking for content - and an audience

For many, the technical challenge of setting up a website is pleasure enough. The result on screen might be pedestrian, but at least it's there. But the decision about what to display is

the hardest of all. Be jealous of the woman with the world's second largest collection of miniature whiskey bottles. She already has content, images in the making, structure, and, probably, an audience. Be very jealous of the guy with two hundred schemes for reducing your income tax bill. He has compelling text, step-by-step examples and, potentially, a lucrative enterprise (although thousands of failed commercial ventures had the same belief). If you resemble neither of these characters, start with a more readily available subject: your family, your work or your hobby. Alternatively, you could research your ancestry and consider building an interactive family tree – we'll cover all this and more in our projects.

But who will see your site? Assuming you have some text on your pages, the search engines (see page 19) will eventually find you. You can speed up the process by registering your site with some of the major search engines, but you won't find yourself coming up on a search immediately. There's a 'chicken and egg' issue here: many search engines rank pages partly according to how often they've been accessed, but nobody will have accessed yours if they can't find it! You're more likely to attract an audience, or 'traffic', as web professionals like to call it, by publicizing your site to web users with similar interests. Search for sites on a similar topic to yours, and ask their owners for a 'link swap': they'll add a link to your site from theirs (maybe in a list on a 'Links' page), and you add one to theirs from yours.

Setting your sights

Start with pen and paper. Draw four small boxes in a line and imagine what you'd like to see in each. The first one inevitably becomes a kind of title page and leads on to page two. That's

The Robinsons' Family Reunion
Woodsmill Park, Sunday September 7th

Mum & Dad   Our grandchildren   Our friends   The food!

In a few pages' time you'll be able to build a website like this...

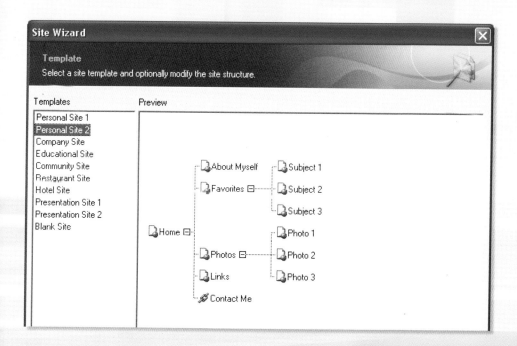

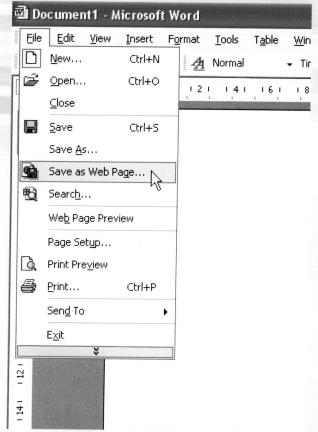

Left: A visual web design package such as Namo WebEditor 6 will help you work out the structure of your pages using a tree diagram. You can see (and change) at a glance what connects to what, and plan the ways that users will be able to navigate your site.
Below: If you have a recent version of Microsoft Word, you'll find that you can turn a basic word processor document into a simple web page. It's not an ideal solution, but it's one way to start. Just select *Save as Web Page* from the file menu (or *Save as HTML,* depending on the version).

where the similarity to a book ends abruptly, because there's no reason why page three should follow two. You can give users the choice of jumping straight to page four if the prospect of page three doesn't thrill them. Pretty soon you'll have lots of pages, with arrows linking them in a tangle of lines. This is the time to make decisions about scope and content, long before concerning yourself with the actual design of your home on the web (again, see the projects to find out more). Aim for six pages or fewer as a first attempt – it's easy to add more as you develop the site. That's the beauty of the web.

A thought for the user

This is also a good time to consider the eventual viewer of your site. If you already use the Internet, you'll know the tedium of waiting ages for a web page to download, or of long scrolling pages filled with repetitive text. Then there's the frustration of finding no way back to the home page due to the absence of links, or links that just don't work. Try to resolve these issues at the outset. Estimate the number of words on a typical page, and establish relevant links between sections. Some web design programs help you do this, but it's just as good with pen and paper. It may look rough, but it will save all kinds of pain later – for you and for your visitors.

The Projects

OK, we've done the science bit! Now all you need is to get your imagination fired up, boot up your computer, make yourself comfortable, and try out these easy-to-follow, fun projects that will give your memories a whole new lease of life. Let's turn your scissors and paste scrapbook into an interactive experience for you, your family, and friends to enjoy, wherever in the world they might be...

BEFORE YOU START...
Not all of the equipment below is absolutely essential, but to get the most out of the projects in this book, you will need:

- A Windows PC (Windows 98 up to Windows XP), or any Apple Macintosh computer running Mac OS 9 or preferably OS X. A good word-processing program, such as Microsoft Word, would be an advantage. If you have the full Microsoft Office suite, then so much the better – and a CD or DVD writer would really put you ahead of the game.
- A digital camera, or a good quality conventional camera and an image scanner. If you've got a video camera, especially a digital one, then you'll get the most out of the later projects.
- A basic image-editing program, such as Adobe Photoshop Elements, Paint Shop Pro, or similar (we'll tell you the options).
- A basic website-building program, such as HotDog, WebEditor, or similar (we'll tell you what to do if you don't have this).
- Loads of imagination, some ideas, and all the old photos, memorabilia, souvenirs, and mementoes you can find!
- Oh... and that Internet connection! Got it all? Here we go...

A holiday album

Let's dive straight into a rich photo resource. What's the best holiday you've ever had? Where are the pictures? Let's hope you didn't forget your camera – and that you know where your old-style album is! Your collection, whether it's carefully organized with every picture captioned and dated, or stacked in an old grocery box, is a priceless treasury of memories. In this project we'll give you the key to unlock it – to transform these ready-made images into a new experience, an album that will delight its viewers all over again. This first project is about giving you an insight into the qualities of a good picture. Why is it that some images tell a story while others stare dumbly back at you? How come some pictures work well in combination, while others need to be on their own?

Many billions of photographs have been taken since the invention of photography. That's generally credited to the Frenchman Nicéphore Niepcé, but the most significant pioneer of photography as we know it today was William Henry Fox Talbot, who was spurred into action by a holiday experience. His companions were all accomplished artists, recording everything in sketchbooks, while he could only look through the lens of a 'camera obscura' and attempt to trace around what he saw. Some 150 years later, his and Niepcé's technology allows all of us to capture the moment without effort.

Beached!
This one has it all. Surprise, humour, good composition, varied texture, harmonious colour, creative viewpoint. If you have even a few pictures like this, your project will be a snap.

THE IMPORTANCE OF VIEWPOINT

Most conventional cameras sit naturally in the hands with the shutter button under the right forefinger, the right eye looking through the viewfinder and the left hand adjusting focus. That's why the great majority of photographs end up in landscape format, shot from eye level. This can be great – but it can also be boring. It's natural to want to include as much as possible in every shot, but the result can be a picture with no point of emphasis. A show without a star.

The plain vanilla shot: there's plenty of detail but nothing leaps out to grab you. Put this one in the 'back in the basement' pile.

The chocolate-chip shot: getting in close, or zooming if you're nervous, produces a far more exciting image.

Warm Horizons

A good example of when to let nature take its course: the faraway shot that works. Bold stripes of colour and a strong sense of scale, all wrapped in spectacular evening light.

Back to the Future

Forget the old instruction books: there are moments when the back view is best. You can almost feel the waves around your toes, inviting you to join the rush to the sea. But have these guys got cold feet?

Close Up and Personal

Is this the yard of beach next to your foot, or an aerial shot of strange mountain ranges? This miniature landscape has much of the fascination of the full-size version. You can use details like this creatively, as we'll explore later...

If you don't yet own a digital camera, consider investing in one: prices are falling, and you'll find it easy to gather and store thousands of images for posterity. If you own one already, you may have a collection of holiday pictures that cry out to be displayed to their best advantage. But if you are still in the foothills of making that decision, your raw materials for now will be your existing prints, slides – perhaps even video footage (see page 76 for ways to get results out of the moving image).

As well as conventional images like these, you can use all the other bits and pieces that you've probably saved to remind you of that special time. Look for postcards, theatre programmes, travel tickets, and tags. See over the page for an example of how you can add these items to your digital photo scrapbook, and turn your ephemera into something more permanent. This project aims to reassemble a number of existing album pictures and print them out as complete sheets. There are several practical considerations that may influence the choice of images from an existing album. Very old pictures stored in unfavourable conditions can suffer from blemishes of various kinds. Some of the problems your old pictures might have are: mould; discolouration due to glue staining through the back of the print; damage on the front through being stuck to other prints or to the album leaves themselves; fading of the image due to sun exposure or insufficient chemical fixing when first made; brown staining from iron oxide in the album or the print substrate; all the way through to scribbling marks made by disrespectful relatives. All these faults can be cured, or at least improved, using the digital techniques outlined in Project Six, and on pages 142 and 143.

Transferring from a digital camera
If your camera contains a removable memory device like a CompactFlash, SmartMedia, or MemoryStick storage card, you can insert the card into a reader, which then plugs into a port (usually the USB slot) on your computer, and download the pictures to your hard disk. There is often a cable alternative linking the camera and computer directly. If the camera only has a fixed internal memory, you'll need to use the cable method.

Just place the print on the scanner, then rev up your software engines…

Scanning existing pictures
Very good results can be obtained using an ordinary desktop scanner. In fact, you will often be able to improve the appearance of old pictures with just a few adjustments, either in the scanner's own software, or afterwards in an image-editing program.

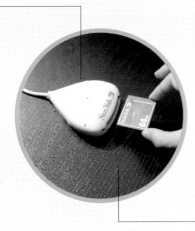

You can store dozens of images on any of the memory cards or sticks that come with some digital still and video cameras. Then just slot into the reader and... you're off.

Ah, springtime in Paris. With help from your scanner software, it's brighter and more colourful than ever.

Those of you who have never stolen hotel soap should skip over these pages. In this project, you can use your holiday 'ephemera' such as travel tickets, souvenir bookmarks, sunglasses, keyfobs, and guidebooks to complement your photographs. Your scanner can deal with shallow three-dimensional objects, although you shouldn't chance its glass surface with large chunks of Uluru or the Grand Canyon. On the other hand, items like that can make handy targets for close-up photography with your digital (or conventional) camera to give your scrapbook a real sense of place. The more you travel the world, the more you'll see that local graphic designs and typography reflect the countries and cities you visit: the chic lettering on the shopping bags from your trip down the Champs Élysées, for example; the bright, sunny colours from your West Country beach holiday...

To further blur the edges between your photos and the local culture of your holiday destination, why not try inserting one into the other? Scan the front page of the local newspaper you picked up and use an image-editing program to add your family members, and revise the headlines to announce your arrival in town. The techniques to do this are basically the same as the retouching tricks you need to work on faulty pictures (which we'll deal with throughout the book).

Look at the size of the items at your disposal and enlarge or reduce them dramatically. For example, you can use the airline tag from your suitcase as an all-over background for a whole album page. Make a pattern out of those left-over banknotes, coins, and unspent traveller's cheques. The door is open wide for the enthusiastic scanner operator!

Above: **Clean Up!**
If there are specks of dust on your scan or on your original, or if the original picture has been damaged in some way, you can use some of the repair tools and filters in Photoshop Elements to fix them. *Dust & Scratches*; *Restore Damaged Photo*; *Red Eye* and *Quick Fix* (for contrast and so on) are just some of the options.

Uluru on a Shoestring
Small objects can be scanned and turned into a digital image you can use like any other, or a background texture for a page.

Colouring Monochrome Graphics
Maybe your album page is a little light on colourful items. It's easy to change dull bits of newsprint, for example, into brilliantly coloured gems. All that's needed is some contrast between the tones in the original. Select one shade of grey in an image-editing program, and fill it with vermilion; select another grey and fill with turquoise. With digital techniques, the options are limitless.

Right: There are two routes to producing a complex collage like this. Route One has you arranging your items in perfect order on the scanner, taking care to overlap each one and, much more difficult than it might seem, getting them absolutely at right angles relative to the edges of the scanner glass. Assuming you can keep things organized (and remember, your images need to be face down, not face up!), it's just one scan and you're done. Route Two, though longer, is recommended. Put two or three items together on the glass, close but not touching, and scan them as a group or, if your scanner/software combination will allow, as separate items. Separate scans will allow you to change the size of each item, giving you much more flexibility when assembling the collage. Following this method, you can assemble the scans layer by layer in your image-editing program, retouch them individually as required, and add shadows for that final, lifelike look.

Now for the easy bit. The pictures have been downloaded or scanned, sized, cropped, retouched, and·stand ready for your final layout. With your computer, you have more than enough flexibility to change their relative sizes; but remember that scanned photos can always be quickly rescanned if they run out of definition under extreme enlargement. This is the moment to try any combination of pictures that appeals to your eye. You can try formal and informal layouts; you can overlap or not overlap; use vignettes and shadows. Liberated from the usual album constraints of glue pot, sticky corners, and rectangular picture shapes of fixed size and format, you are free to decide, change your mind, then decide again. You have all the possibilities of the newsstand magazine designer, with none of the deadlines. Take your time to swap the layers around. Keep back the picture that doesn't quite work, and store it for use in another layout. You'll begin to make judgments about what works well, and what doesn't. Developing this kind of selection process is vital groundwork for moving onto webpages and even more complex presentations. And we'll get on to those soon enough!

CHOOSING PAPER

As we've mentioned before, glossy 'photo' papers offer the most saturated colours with inkjet printers, but tend to be expensive. Quite a bit of trial and error may be necessary before you find a brand that suits your eye and your pocket. Some cheaper papers skimp on the coating process; the worst offenders will show ugly bands of varying density. Your printer software will usually offer different settings for various kinds of paper, and adjust the ink flow automatically to get the best result. At the top end of the price range, you'll find inkjet-suitable 'watercolour' papers, which come from the same mills where the regular artists' version is produced. Other unusual surfaces include imitation silk on a plastic sheet.

Resolution

Above: Your printer probably offers 'draft' quality for speed and economy. The number of dots of ink is reduced and the print-head moves rapidly across the paper surface. The trade-off may sometimes be acceptable, but most times you'll want to stick to high resolution for printed work.

Playing it Straight

The traditional rectangular layout (*above left*) needs strong images like this to keep the eye interested. A small vignette provides good contrast.

The Layered Effect

Angled pictures must be handled with care. Borders and backgrounds help make both these sets of images work together, giving a real sense of place to bring back those precious memories.

Now that you have your pictures selected, enhanced where necessary, and composited into single sheets with vignettes, drop shadows, applied textures, and scanned memorabilia, it's a good time to consider the final format and style of your newly revamped, conventional scrapbook. If you buy a commercial product, these decisions are mostly made for you. Depending on your budget you can choose padded covers, gold blocking, elaborate interleaving, even an integral musical box (if that's to your taste). In theory you could use any kind of blank book.

If you're a practical person, it's not hard to construct an album of your own. Imagine you have some stunning panorama shots. It's a crime to stick them across two pages with a gap in the middle. Why not mount your panoramas back-to-back on thin cardboard? Then make matching front and back covers on heavier cardboard, and get the local print or copy shop to bind the whole production together. They can generally offer plastic comb binding (not very beautiful, but effective and strong), Wire-O (more elegant, and more expensive), or, if you only have a few prints, a simple slide-on plastic spine. If you prefer to do the whole job yourself, be careful with that Scotch tape: your efforts will look a whole lot better after 20 years without a garland of semi-liquid gloop.

TELLING THE TALE OF YOUR HOLIDAY

The secret of this first, easy project – and of digital scrapbooking techniques in general – is to choose, edit, and compile images that really tell the story of your holiday. So, page one could be leaving home, the trip to the airport, the luggage – and the inevitable wait. Move on to page two and you've arrived exhausted at your destination, probably hours late and yearning for the comfort of your hotel room. Keep the tickets if you can, the menu at the hotel, a napkin or two, maybe even that vital 'Do Not Disturb' sign in six languages. All will take on a life of their own once you've scanned them, edited and composited them in your image-editing program. Then it's straight on to the main event: those days on the beach; the local bars and restaurants; the guide books and souvenirs; those few secretly taken snapshots of family members as they complained about the service. It's your story!

Preserving your Work

Once you've composed a few pages of pictures, put your drop shadows in place, and maybe scanned some textures or found objects, it's time to start compiling your new, improved, yet still traditional album. Why not try canvas-textured paper for an economical 'fine-art' look. Or make two moves in your image-editing program: use the *Watercolour* function to give a painterly effect over the whole layout, then choose *Canvas Texture* as an overall filter.

Lickety-stick

Who remembers lick-and-stick photo corners? The modern way is to protect the prints under a thin transparent sheet. As a bonus, static electricity holds them firmly in position. Avoid albums with actively adhesive sheets of any kind – every bit of lint you ever saw will be preserved forever.

The family event @ home page

Take your place on the worldwide stage with this fun-to-do family Web project. Whether you delve into your store of existing images or set up a whole new event just to be sure of getting the shots you want, creating this kind of record is an ideal way of honing your picture-making skills. You select the shots, you direct the layout, you mastermind the order of events – and with our help you can overcome the technical challenges of assembling your first scrapbook and uploading it to the Internet. It's easy!

Digital technology can help you bring your family pictures to life on the Internet, and that's what we're going to do with this project. But first, there's some more technical stuff to get through before we move deeper into the projects...

We've looked at the basic technical issues surrounding websites in our introduction. But what about the software? If you wanted to, you could learn HTML, but these days there is no need to do this: a whole host of programs will write the code for you 'behind the scenes', and you need never know what it looks like, or what it does. But if you're keen to find out, the big screen of code *opposite* is what HTML is really like.

If you have Microsoft Office installed, many of the programs in the suite have a *Save as Web Page* function. Take Word, for example. You can turn just about any document prepared in Word, which might include photos and graphics, into an HTML document (your own web page) and publish it on the Internet, burn it onto a CD, or email it to your friends. It's easy! There are dozens of other options, but let's talk Word first.

The Secret Code

Lurking behind every web page is a secret code, called HTML, which describes how each element of a page appears (and tells your browser where to find other elements, like graphics or sound files). Here it is... ugh!

```
index.html - Notepad
File  Edit  Format  View  Help
<html>
<head>
<title>%namo-title%</title>
<meta name="generator" content="N
<meta name="author" content="John
<style>
<!--
body { color:rgb(0,0,0); font-f
h1 { color:rgb(128,64,0); font-si
h2 { color:rgb(128,0,0); font-siz
-->
</style>
<meta http-equiv="content-type" co
<script language="JavaScript">
<!--
function na_preload_img()
{
  var img_list = na_preload_img.
  if (document.preloadlist == nu
    document.preloadlist = new Ar
  var top = document.preloadlist.
  for (var i=0; i < img_list.leng
    document.preloadlist[top+i] =
    document.preloadlist[top+i].s
  }
}

// --></script>
</head>

<body bgcolor="#FF8000" text="bla
<div align="left">
    <table border="0" width="750";
      <tr>
        <td width="744"><font
<div align="center">
<img src="nav/nav_1_index_bhb.gif"
border="0" class="namo-banner" al
<!--NAMO_NAVBAR_END--></font></td:
      </tr>
      <tr>
        <td width="744">
          <p><font size="2";
        </td>
      </tr>
      <tr>
        <td width="744"><!--N
<div align="center">
<a href="index.html"
onmouseover="na_change_img_src('n
onmouseout="na_restore_img_src('n
border="0" class="namo-button2" a
onmouseover="na_change_img_src('n
onmouseout="na_restore_img_src('n
border="0" class="namo-button2" a
onmouseover="na_change_img_src('n
onmouseout="na_restore_img_src('n
```

The Robinsons' Family Reunion
Woodsmill Park, Sunday September 7th

Mum & Dad   Our grandchildren   Our friends   The food!

```
"text

k=")                    ali

5"><!--    _NAVBAR_START B

"nav_index_BHO"
" align="texttop"></div>


</font></p>


BAR_START T H C h      -1 0

x_THO', 'document', 'nav/nav_          _          g  ,     
x_THO', 'document')"><img src="nav/nav_6_index_btn_home.gif" name="nav_index_THO"
ne" align="texttop"></a><a href="profile.html"
x_TH1', 'document', 'nav/nav_6_profile_thr.gif', true)"
x_TH1', 'document')"><img src="nav/nav_6_profile_th.gif" name="nav_index_TH1"
ut Myself" align="texttop"></a><a href="favorite.html"
x_TH2', 'document', 'nav/nav_6_favorite_thr.gif', true)"
x_TH2', 'document')"><img src="nav/nav_6_favorite_th.gif" name="nav_index_TH2"
```

Once you've produced a page in Word, simply select *Save as Web Page* or *Save as HTML* from the *File* menu. You can then open this document in your Web browser (Explorer, Navigator, Safari, or one of the various good alternatives, such as Opera, at *www.opera.com*). Of course, the document still sits on your computer – it's not yet on the Internet. We'll show you how to post it online in a few pages' time.

If you want to see what the HTML version of your document looks like for yourself, simply select *View Source* while the page is displayed in your browser and you'll see a screen full of HTML that the program has written for you behind the scenes.

Using this technique (in Word, you'll also need to select *Online Layout* from the *View* menu) you can quickly transform simple documents into effective web pages – but bear in mind that some of the familiar Word features can't be used. Multi-column newspaper-style layouts, for example, won't transfer to HTML. There are plus points as well, though: you can select a range of background colours and patterns that aren't available as standard for word processor documents.

Exporting from Word is a quick way to put something online, but to lay out a site properly you'll need a dedicated web design program. HotDog (*www.sausage.com*) and Namo WebEditor (*www.namo.com*) are relatively cheap and easy to use; Microsoft FrontPage (*www.microsoft.com*) and NetObjects Fusion (*www.netobjects.com*) are more ambitious; and for the professionals there's Macromedia Dreamweaver and Adobe GoLive. Even the more basic packages are fun to use and will probably take you as far as you ever need to go. Many of these programs can be downloaded as free trial versions, and you can also pick up free or trial packages on computer magazines' cover-mounted CDs.

There are lots of other ways to build a site. The Netscape browser has an optional program called Composer, with which you can build simple web pages. At Moonfruit (*www.moonfruit.com*) you can make a site within your own browser in an hour or two, without any extra software. There's a small monthly fee to 'host' your site on the Internet, but you can try out the service for free. Mac users with a subscription to Apple's Mac service (*www.mac.com*) can build a site using the HomePage feature.

OK, now let's turn your family event into a fun, interactive scrapbook that will give your photos a new lease of life!

You've Seen How the Experts Do It...

You've watched Google search for web pages, pictures... even direct you to websites that let you track down long-lost friends. But why not make your own home page, or website, that brings those friends to you?

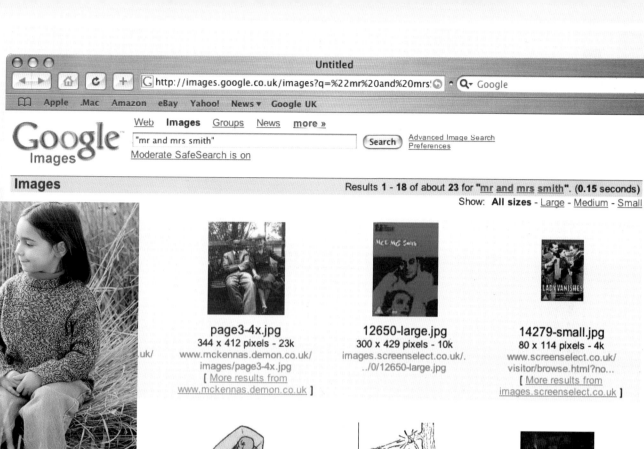

Untitled

http://images.google.co.uk/images?q=%22mr%20and%20mrs'

Google

Apple .Mac Amazon eBay Yahoo! News ▾ Google UK

Google Images

Web **Images** Groups News **more »**

"mr and mrs smith"

Moderate SafeSearch is on

[Search] Advanced Image Search
Preferences

Images

Results **1 - 18** of about **23** for "mr and mrs smith". **(0.15 seconds)**

Show: **All sizes** - Large - Medium - Small

page3-4x.jpg
344 x 412 pixels - 23k
www.mckennas.demon.co.uk/
images/page3-4x.jpg
[More results from
www.mckennas.demon.co.uk]

12650-large.jpg
300 x 429 pixels - 10k
images.screenselect.co.uk/.
../0/12650-large.jpg

14279-small.jpg
80 x 114 pixels - 4k
www.screenselect.co.uk/
visitor/browse.html?no...
[More results from
images.screenselect.co.uk]

salsa_band.jpg
200 x 150 pixels - 6k
w.cubancyclechallenge.co.uk/
cuba_party.html

26.gif
37 x 66 pixels - 2k
www.blackstar.co.uk/
video/year/1941/j:L

41

Don't say a word! If your intended subjects – family, friends or colleagues – suspect that they are about to become raw material for your web project, you may well get an icy reaction. Although there are few people who still believe the camera can steal the soul, many get irritable when being stage-managed. What you need is that most difficult combination: organized spontaneity. Dilute your presence as camera-person by inviting a crowd, setting up games and distractions, even getting a friend to act as a decoy photographer while you skulk around the edges catching people off guard. Clearly, none of this subterfuge is necessary if your subjects are natural actors, craving the adoring gaze of the camera.

To establish the sequence, try to get a really wide shot of the scene, ideally before the fun starts (the calm before the storm?), making a handy contrast to the shot of everyone departing at the end. Shoot the invitation if there is one – or if you made it on the computer, save a copy from your graphics program as a JPEG image, or bring it up on-screen and take a 'screen grab'. In Windows, press the PrtScrn key, then open your photo editor and make a new image from the Clipboard. On a Mac, press Command-Shift-4 and draw around an area of the screen to store it on your Desktop with the name 'Picture 1'.

When things get started, you'll have to rely on your natural cunning to get the best shots. Try to shoot everyone, since, in spite of their denials, no-one likes to be left out. Get someone to shoot you, for the same reason. Shoot people doing something, even if it's only gesturing impatiently at you. Shoot from above; lie down and get a shot from the ground; shoot through trees, windows and doors; shoot against the light; shoot the food and drink, and the kids at play; capture the adults in deep conversation, and don't forget the pets (they'll be far less self-conscious).

If you're shooting digitally and are sure that these pictures will only be used on the web project, set the camera to its lowest quality. This will normally give enough resolution for a web page at 72 dots per inch, and you'll get many more shots into your camera's memory.

Getting Down to It
You'll be lucky to get a shot like this. Corn cobs and skewers rarely line up so neatly, and it's hard to get the people to do the same. Try, but don't get sunburned or sizzled by the barbecue.

Where's the Sun?
Try to break the old rule about having the sun immediately behind you. Faces look better when not in full sun. Eyes don't pucker up. And sometimes you get a bonus of a backlit halo of hair or a hat. Ah... a star is born.

Get in Close

Make it a priority to get some good food shots. And get in before the ketchup starts to fly!

The Aaah Factor

If you find this type of picture too sentimental for your project, maybe it will still work as your Christmas card, or as a calendar picture (see page 52).

Action is Everything

Lots of light, quick thinking, and a fast shutter speed gets you the reward. If you're using a digital camera, you can check the screen immediately to see if you hit the spot. If not, they might do it all over again. Some medical authorities reckon that holding children this way, though fun, is a bad idea.

Back at home in the calm glow of your monitor, it's time to review your harvest of pictures. If you've shot on conventional film, this selection procedure is especially important. There's no point in scanning stacks of prints that you know in your bones are never going to make it. If you've been shooting digitally, there's still a selection to be made. If you can't face the idea of trashing anything, then burn a CD (see page 90), or make some other form of backup. That way you can have the luxury of changing your mind right through the process.

In either case, you may find it useful to sort the pictures into groups on-screen. You could make folders called simply 'Start', 'Middle' and 'End', for example. Soon you'll have another folder called 'Odd', and another one called 'Email' containing pictures so hilarious that they won't wait to be turned into a web page, but have to be emailed *right now*.

LOSE THAT WEIGHT/WAIT

Welcome to the hard realities of image compression. The same law that makes your digital camera run more quickly on its low-quality setting means that web pictures have to be slimmed down to load quickly. There are several ways this can be done. Your digital camera probably compresses its pictures automatically into JPEG format ('Joint Photographic Experts Group', pronounced 'jay-peg'). Your scanner probably produces TIFFs (Tagged Image File Format, acronym fans). Your image-editing software can deal with both of these and others such as GIF (Graphics Interchange Format). The quest is to make the picture file as small as possible without losing too much quality. The main tool is trial and error. The process is known as 'optimization', though it often feels like 'leastworstification'. But that's the classic trade-off between quality and file size that the Internet creates. Deal with it!

Another file format is GIF (Graphics Interchange Format), which deals mostly with images containing significant areas of flat colour. So JPEG is likely to be your main weapon. First, establish the required size of the image (it's always measured in pixels, since you're dealing now with screen display). Then choose the amount of compression, moving the slider from low to high, hit *OK* when you're happy, and it's ready to take its place on-screen. When you see it again, it will have a '.jpg' tag (extension).

The Quality/File Size Trade-off

Whenever you save an image for the web, you'll need to get the file size down, so it doesn't take an age to load. This means losing some quality by 'compressing' the data. One option is to let Photoshop Elements make settings to achieve a desired size – or close to it.

Saving Face

The original portrait *left* has a lot of subtle colours and a wide contrast range. The lit areas of the hat are completely white, and the pupils utterly black.

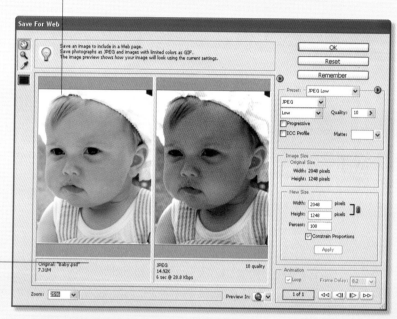

Trying too Hard

In the program window *above,* the original can be examined closely alongside a preview of the optimized version. Choosing 'JPEG Low', though it makes a small and speedy file, is obviously wrong – the image begins to fill with ugly blocks that invade the light areas. You'll need to up the quality a bit – but watch that file size!

On the Edge

This solution (*JPEG Medium*, or 30 in the *Quality* dialog) is a good compromise between small file size and clarity. You don't have to know about file sizes and what they mean: a useful measure is to keep an eye on the timing note at the bottom of the optimization screen. This shows how long the picture would take to download via the (very) average modem. How long would *you* wait?

Now you have it all: a plan (remember those pencil sketches?); the picture selection all resized and optimized; some spare pictures in case the first selection needs amending; an idea about the words and maybe a background colour scheme. Make sure all the pictures are in the same location on the computer to save needless navigation, and plunge in. You can try all this out without having any web space of your own. Just set your browser to work 'offline' and you can develop a miniature website like this completely independently of the Internet. You could equally well send the project to a friend by 'attaching' the files to an email, or burn them onto CD. To actually 'publish' your pages, however, you need web space and a small piece of software which sends or 'posts' them to the Internet. So, another set of initials: FTP (for File Transfer Protocol). This software takes your files directly to your web space, and allows you to pull them down again whenever necessary for updating. There's normally a password system to prevent others interfering with your space. Some web design programs and browsers have the FTP routine built in, but if not, there are freeware versions like Fetch and Transmit (for the Mac) or CuteFTP which do the job just as well.

In any web page program, there'll be a sample site. Look at the way it's put together, then try substituting your own pictures in their place.

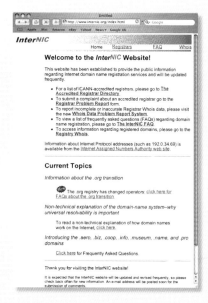

A Web Address of Your Own

www.internic.org is the place to track down web authorities from which you can buy a domain (Internet address) of your own. Try it out, and follow the simple instructions you'll find there.

Greetings from the Country

Here's what you're aiming for: a simple, colourful home page that can take your friends and family (the ones you didn't invite) right there to your day in the park or the country. Simple links to each section will allow you to display your pictures topic by topic, and your visitors to navigate quickly.

The Robinsons' Family Reunion
Woodsmill Park, Sunday September 7th

<u>Mum & Dad</u>   <u>Our grandchildren</u>   <u>Our friends</u>   The food!

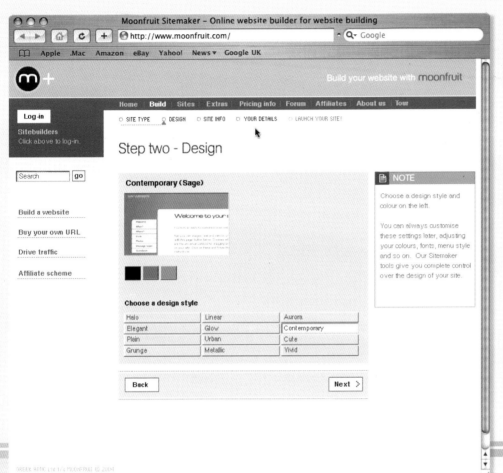

How do I make a vignette?
See page 53
How do I make a link?
See page 64

The Moonfruit has Landed

If website-building software is too much of a giant leap, then take one small step by going to *www.moonfruit.com*. This is a simple online service where you can build a website in an hour or two. It's easy, and you don't need programming skills or software. There's a small monthly fee to show your site to the world.

PAGES, PAGES, PAGES GALORE

For your first Web project, keep it simple: just half a dozen pages or so. These will be enough to get a flavour of the event online – or onto a CD or an email attachment – and you can add or subtract as many pages as you like later. But for any of these projects, it's a good idea to test your web page in more than one browser. Don't assume everyone has the same browser as you, because web pages have a nasty habit of appearing differently in different browsers, as we mentioned in the introduction: Netscape, Internet Explorer (often known as 'IE'), Safari, and other browsers work in slightly different ways. Follow the simple instructions in your web design software about naming files and putting them in the right places, and you'll soon be creating simple web pages like these, left and right. Don't forget to link to the other pages from your home page.

A pet calendar

How old's your dog in dog years? When's her birthday? And when do your cat's nine lives begin all over again? (Don't forget that visit to the vet's tomorrow!) Paper-based calendars aren't just useful for keeping track of important dates and events, they make an ideal foil for your favourite prints. But when those calendars are digital and interactive, a whole world of possibilities opens up – you can edit them, reuse them next year with new dates, even print them onto posters, bed linen, or crockery (we'll show you how to do this later!)

Many image-editing applications provide templates for creating calendars, and simply by working through a step-by-step process you can use these to produce customized calendars featuring your favourite shots. Photoshop Elements 3 is one good example. From its 'Creations', choose Wall Calendar. You'll find a variety of formats on offer, each with the option of a title page and/or captions for each image. If you start your Creation while in Organizer mode, the images currently displayed are automatically imported into the calendar; otherwise, you can add selected shots from your Catalogue. Either way, you're then shown which image will appear with each month, and swapping them around is just a matter of clicking and dragging. Elements also warns you if any of your pics lack the resolution to come out well when your calendar is printed. Type a title, add your captions, and all that remains is to save your calendar as a PDF file, which you can print out or email to any friend or relation with a PC or Mac. And all in two shakes of a dog's tail.

GETTING RID OF UNWANTED DETAILS
If your pet photos are ready to use just as they come, count yourself very lucky! Getting our furry friends to behave for the camera, let alone to pose, can be well-nigh impossible. So many of your photos will need a little retouching prior to inclusion. Removing details – such as a steadying hand or foot (as here), or a distracting background – will make your pictures more imposing. On the next page you can see how this shot was given more focus – by blurring it.

Create a Wall Calendar

Step 2: Arrange Your Pho

Add Photos...   Use Photo Aga

Remove Photo

Feb

Mar

Apr

Jul

Aug

Sep

Nov

Dec

The Cat's Whiskers

Photoshop Elements 3 includes a Wall Calendar maker that can generate calendars for any set of months you choose – not just the usual January to December. Import enough pictures to fill the spaces available, then use this handy display to set which pet appears each month. Yellow triangles mean the image resolution isn't up to the job, but you're free to ignore them if you just can't resist that shot of Rover that you grabbed with your mobile phone.

Learn More About: Creating a Wall Calendar

[< Previous Step]   [Next Step >]   [Cancel]

Before you paste your pet pictures into a calendar, there's plenty you can do to make them look even better. Remember that you – or anyone you give the calendar to – will be looking at the photo for a whole month, so there'll be plenty of opportunities for criticism!

One of the best ways to emphasize the subject of your photo is to remove the surrounding background, especially if your pet's not known for its tidiness. Image-editing applications provide several ways of achieving this effect. Two of the cleverest are Adobe Photoshop's *Extract* command, which sadly isn't included in Photoshop Elements, and *Background Eraser*, which is (*right*).

A more basic alternative, found in almost all image applications, is the *Lasso* tool. You can use this to draw around the edge of the subject. Since few of us have hands steady enough to draw an accurate outline with a pencil, let alone a mouse, some programs – including Elements – provide a variation called the *Magnetic Lasso*. Rather than relying on your freehand technique, this attaches itself to the edge of your subject automatically as you draw – roughly – around it. It's far from foolproof (it can be confused when there's more than one edge to follow), but with a little practice you can achieve very effective results indeed. And we'll bet there've been times when you wanted to lasso your pet...

If you have a pet with a *very* fluffy coat, you may find neither of these methods is able to select every hair. Professional photo retouchers use add-ons such as Corel KnockOut in these cases, but it's unlikely to be worth your while investing in such a specialist tool. Instead, try a method – such as those below – that doesn't rely on a perfect outline.

IMAGE EXTRACTION

You can get rid of a distracting background using Photoshop Elements' Background Eraser. Here it is in action. You'll find the tool in the main toolbox along with the ordinary Eraser (click and hold the icon to pop out the alternatives). Select it and you get a cursor consisting of a circle with a cross in the middle. The basic idea is that when you click with the mouse, it deletes everything within the circle that isn't the same colour as the cross. So as long as the cross doesn't touch your subject (here, the dog), it won't get erased, while the background will. Continue around the edge to get a complete outline, and you can then use other tools such as Lasso to remove the background beyond this.

Blurring the background (and the foot!) has focused attention on the subject, not your footwear.

OTHER EFFECTS

Image extraction isn't the only way to emphasize the subject of your photo. Soft edges, blurring effects and even colour changes can all help create a more effective image. In the case of the cat (right) we've applied a Grain filter to give a textured finish to the photo. For the picture of the dog (far right) we've used the Lasso tool again, but then blurred the background. For a final flourish we've also applied a vignette (see page 52) to soften the edges.

Paws for thought? This combination of grainy and soft edge effects adds character to our canny cat.

The *Background Eraser* and its Options

After you activate the *Background Eraser*, you can set the
Brush Size, Limits and Tolerance in the *Options* toolbar.
Set Limits to *Discontiguous*; switch to Contiguous if you
get holes in your pet! Reduce the Tolerance depending on
how similar the background colour is to the subject.

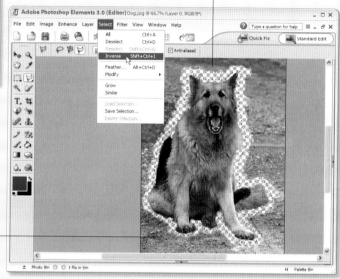

The Extracted Image

Once you've worked all the
way around the subject, use
the *Freehand Selection* tool
(Lasso) to draw roughly
around inside the area you
just erased. Then use *Inverse*
(*Select* menu) so that the
remaining background is
selected. Press Delete
(Windows) or Backspace
(Mac) to remove it. Use the
normal *Eraser* to tidy up any
bits left around the edges.

EXPOSURES WITH CLOSE-UP

**When taking photos of your pets
close up, there can be exposure
problems when using some cameras.
Flash exposure tends to be too great,
resulting in a photo that's overexposed. You can instantly correct
much of this by using the 'quick fix'
or 'auto' enhancements in most
image editors, or simply alter the
brightness and contrast sliders.**

The Elliptical Marquee

Open your image in Elements and choose the *Elliptical Marquee* tool. The *Feather* option sets the softness of the edge of the selection you're going to make.

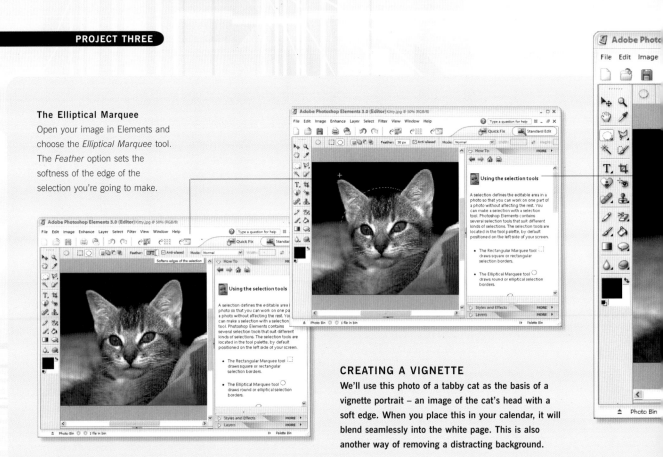

CREATING A VIGNETTE

We'll use this photo of a tabby cat as the basis of a vignette portrait – an image of the cat's head with a soft edge. When you place this in your calendar, it will blend seamlessly into the white page. This is also another way of removing a distracting background.

OTHER SPREADSHEETS

On this page we explain how you might use Microsoft Excel – available as a stand-alone product and as part of Microsoft Office – to make a customized calendar. You could achieve similar results with other spreadsheet applications, such as Lotus 1-2-3 (part of IBM's Lotus SmartSuite), Quattro Pro (found in Corel WordPerfect Office), or the spreadsheet modules in low-cost 'productivity suites' like AppleWorks (on the Mac), StarOffice and Ability Office (for Windows). With most of these packages you can not only lay out your calendar and format the dates as you please, but also enhance your creation with colours, textures, graphics and text effects.

It may surprise you to hear that Excel – the spreadsheet included with Microsoft Office – is a great alternative for calendar production. There are three good reasons why. First, its grid of resizeable 'cells' is perfect for a calendar layout. You could have standard week and month tables, or go for something more avant-garde, such as a frame of days and dates around a central image. Second, it offers lots of date formats and options, and of course extensive calculation abilities – how about a calendar calibrated in dog years? Third, you can use some of the simpler spreadsheet tools to bring your calendar to life – even online on a website (you can save a spreadsheet as HTML). With a bit of imagination, and a basic knowledge of maths, you could set up a few simple calculations. If you divide the average cat's lifespan by nine, how many of its nine lives has yours used up? How long has it been since her last visit to the vet?

Importing images into Excel is as easy as clicking a button on the Picture toolbar. Use this to import your images, trim them (using the

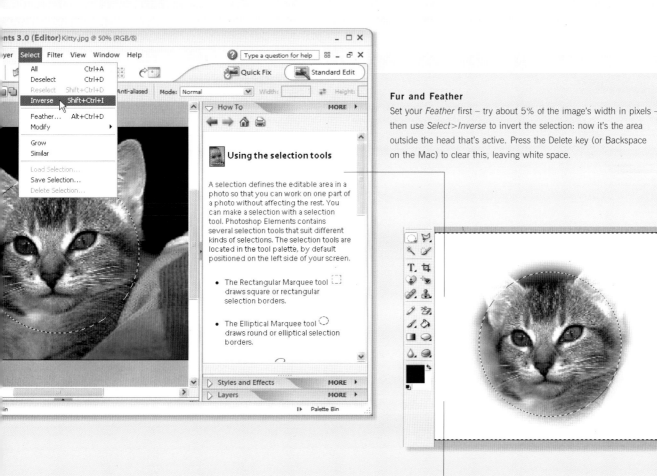

Fur and Feather

Set your *Feather* first – try about 5% of the image's width in pixels – then use *Select>Inverse* to invert the selection: now it's the area outside the head that's active. Press the Delete key (or Backspace on the Mac) to clear this, leaving white space.

Crop command), and make fine adjustments. Once an image has been imported you can use its 'handles' to resize it to fit your calendar layout. Repositioning is equally easy: just click and drag.

It's true that Excel is a professional business tool, and many of its features and concepts are designed for the advanced financial or scientific user. But don't let that put you off – the nature of Excel is such that if you don't need those high-powered tools, you needn't see them! Stick with simple tables and you'll have all the power you need. Then explore the Formatting palette and examine how you can alter the look of your calendar with a change of font or a little colour. Use the Cell Shading feature for those important jab dates!

For colourful or dramatic text (to use as captions or to name the months), give Excel's WordArt a try (*Insert>Picture>WordArt*). Select a WordArt style, type in your text and press *OK* to emblazon your page with text worthy of the local signwriter.

Using your Vignette

When you're happy with the result, save it under a different filename. Import this file into your calendar and see how it looks!

There's another group of applications that's ideal for constructing calendars: page layout software, also known as desktop publishing (DTP) programs. These are the same applications that you'd use to produce your community, club, or society newsletters, and even national magazines and newspapers – as well as books like the one you're reading now. The Big Daddy of DTP is QuarkXPress, which is used to create many of the publications you'll see on the average newsstand. There's little that Quark – as it's generally referred to – can't do, but it's too expensive for most people even to think about. Adobe InDesign is quickly catching up with Quark in popularity and is quite a bit cheaper (especially if you invest in other serious graphics programs, such as Photoshop, at the same time). It also provides more help for beginners. But if you don't need all the professional capabilities, budget packages to consider include Serif PagePlus (*www.serif.com*) (Windows only) and Ready,Set,Go! (*www.diwan.com*), which is available for both Mac and Windows and in editions that support Arabic and other non-Roman written languages.

With page layout applications, especially InDesign, you're far less limited in the way you can mix photos and text. You could have your calendar flowing around the vignette image we created on the previous spread. Or you could fade the image across the page and lay the calendar dates over the top. The only limit is your imagination.

Once you've created your calendar, don't be afraid to share it. It will look great on your wall, but give one to friends at the pet club and await the plaudits! Or link to it from your home page, email them your web address (URL) and wait for the visitors.

TRANSFERRING DATA

Just as Microsoft Word's native data format has become the standard for document exchanges between computers and over the Web, so the Excel format (indicated by the file extension '.xls') has become the standard in spreadsheet exchanges. Even if you don't use Excel, there's a high probability that the application you do use will be able to understand a page from an Excel spreadsheet. Page layout applications tend to be more parochial. If you've used one of these, the best way to save your document for others to see is as a PDF (Adobe Portable Document Format). Note the options to 'optimize' your file either for print, which will make a large file with high-resolution images, or for web/on-screen use, which will make a smaller file.

Seen it All Before?

The toolboxes provided by page layout programs such as Adobe InDesign and Serif PagePlus (*above*) feature many similar tools to those used in image-editing applications. Although getting to grips with every feature could take months, with only a little practice you'll be able to exploit the key features required to create a calendar. All these programs – from QuarkXPress, available for Mac and Windows at huge cost, down to older versions of PagePlus for Windows, which you can get free from *www.freeserifsoftware.com* – have extensive on-screen help and tutorials, and usually some special features to help with tabular layouts.

A Day to Remember

Whatever your pictures show, a few special effects (here we used Photoshop Elements' Diffuse Glow) will make them look special. Your finished calendar will not only be a work of art but a useful tool – or a great gift.

April						2006
Sun	Mon	Tue	Wed	Thu	Fri	Sat
						1
2	3	4	5	6	7	8
9	10	11	12	13	14	15
16	17	18	19	20	21	22
23	24	25	26	27	28	29
30						

Well, the weather's getting warmer -- but who turned the radiators off?

Pass it On

You can print your calendar out or save it as a PDF document, which other users can view and print using Adobe Acrobat Reader software (already installed on most computers). There's even an option to email it straight off.

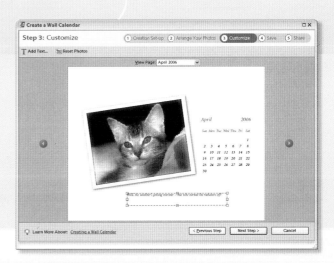

55

Let's move house!
And home page...

How do your friends get to your new house? And how do you tell the story of your day? Moving house scores highly on the stress scale, so photography will probably be the last thing on your mind in the flurry of activity on moving day. But, like all life-changing events, it's full of images that will make most families feel a lot happier about the event once the move is done. The necessary healing interval might be days, weeks, or even years, depending on the success of your particular migration, but you can be sure that a little planning in the pre-move period will bring great rewards. On these pages you'll find many tips that suggest alternatives and enhancements to the regular shots of comings and goings. And one more thing: make double sure that the box labelled 'family photos' gets top priority safe handling. Otherwise you could be reconstructing your family history from other people's albums. And the key to this project, the key to your 'moving home' page, is making something useful that you can email your friends and family members, or publish online. Just email them the web address!

THE HOME PAGE OF YOUR DREAMS
Keep the estate agent's brochure that first attracted you to your new home (the one with the captivating, sunlit picture and the carefully crafted words). If you bought your home through the Internet, download or screen-grab the page. If you're not feeling too happy about your buy, you could always compare the picture that attracted you with one you took of the real thing...

The Right Direction
Whether your new location has pressed steel or top-of-the-range carved stone, make sure you shoot the street sign.

MYRTLE GROVE

livingspaces
SOLD
SUBJECT TO CONTRACT
view by appointment only
tel: 0191 222 1000

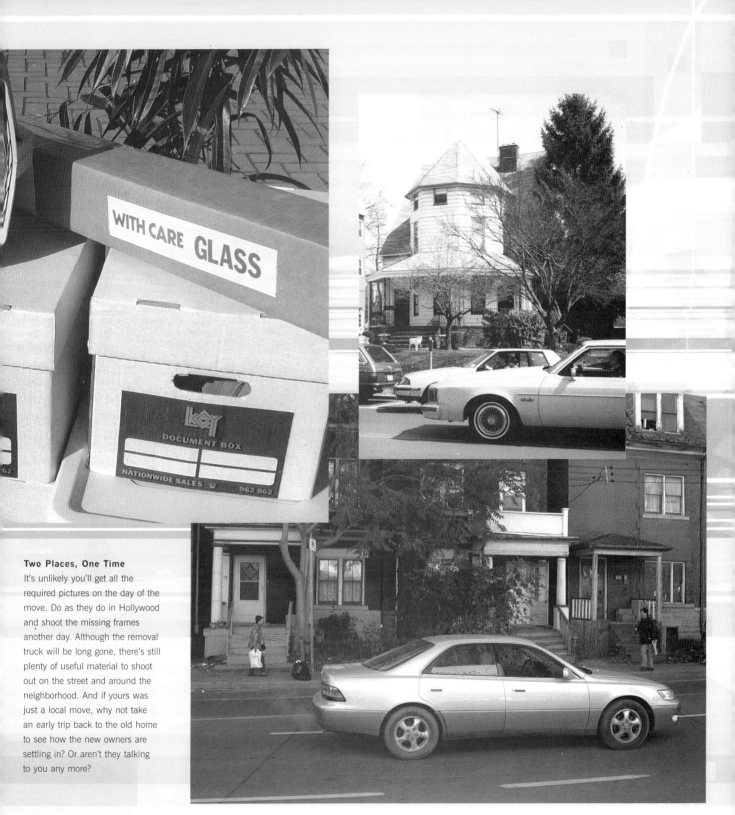

Two Places, One Time

It's unlikely you'll get all the required pictures on the day of the move. Do as they do in Hollywood and shoot the missing frames another day. Although the removal truck will be long gone, there's still plenty of useful material to shoot out on the street and around the neighborhood. And if yours was just a local move, why not take an early trip back to the old home to see how the new owners are settling in? Or aren't they talking to you any more?

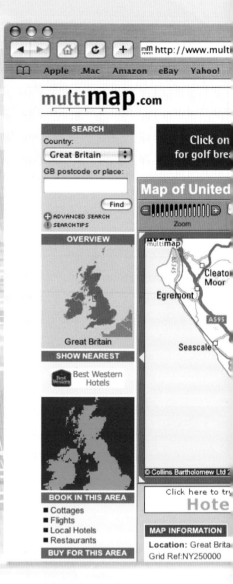

If your move took you to another county – or country – you'll be able to create a real travelogue. Remember that your audience may not be familiar with your new location, or even the old one. So you'll need to look for maps. You may find free local street maps at your new town hall or Tourist Information office. Printed maps, of the kind you buy in stationers' and petrol stations, generally have an excess of detail – there are just too many contour lines and bridle paths. You could trace over them to simplify them, but that would involve the hassle of scanning them, and the area you want is bound to cross over two pages!

Instead, turn to the new breed of Internet mapmakers. Try any of the route-planning websites and you'll see examples of their work. These maps are kept deliberately simple, since they're designed to be viewed, and printed out, at a wide range of sizes. When you zoom right in to an area, the map will change its character completely to show a denser mass of information, with streets and even buildings starting to appear.

It's easy to copy a map by dragging the image from your web browser or doing a screen grab (see page 42). But remember this isn't strictly legal (see below right), so keep it for personal use only.

A QUICK GUIDE TO ONLINE MAP SERVICES

The mind of the mapmaker works in a different way from that of the map user. Where we want to know how many centimetres to the kilometre or miles to the inch, the mapmaker prefers to deal in scale ratios. 500,000:1 – five hundred thousand to one – gives you five kilometres to a centimetre, or around eight miles to the inch (see why we went decimal?). The map *above right* is shown at this scale. Let's say your move was 50 kilometres, and you're looking to fill most of an average-sized web page with a map that covers your start and end locations. So, 50km at 5 kilometres per centimetre gives you 10 centimetres – easily accommodated on-screen, with room to spare at each end. The largest scale normally available in online maps is 5,000:1, which would be ideal for showing your route if you'd just moved around the block!

BEWARE OF COPYRIGHT!

A legal notice on the map site shown here (*www.multimap.com*) points out that you're not allowed to do anything with the maps except look at them within the site in your web browser. For a fee, businesses can licence maps showing their location for use on their own websites. Copyright in maps is heavily protected, so don't be tempted to copy one onto your own home page!

United Kingdom | Multimap.com

map/browse.cgi?client=public&X=3

Google

Google UK

my multi**map** ● Register ● Log in ● Log out ● Help

S | DIRECTIONS | AERIAL PHOTOS | BUSINESS SERVICES | ABOUT US | SITEMAP | HELP

stern
d the UK

Best Western

om

Print | Link | Aerial | Traffic | Book hotels | Buy map | Bigger | Help

LOCAL INFORMATION
Pick or type a category:

--

fault_kw=

OFFERS

Generators
Buy Electricity
Generators Here Low
Prices And Delivery.
www.Top-UK.co.uk

MY MULTIMAP
You are not logged in to
MyMultimap
● Log in here
● Register here

Homing In?

When you finally get your route
in your sights, there'll be a lot
of other items competing. Make
a screen grab of the map alone.

CUMBRIAN MOUNTAIN

Ullswater

Thirlmere

Haweswater
Reservoir

A591

A6

A592

Ambleside

A593

Tel

SEASCALE

Wordsworth Drive

Green Street

Fourth Avenue

SCHOOL

SHOPPING CENTRE

N

Egremont Street

GOLF COURSE

It's time to put some meat on these bare bones. If you have some experience with an image-editing program, you are probably already thinking, 'I can make a better map than the one I've just downloaded', and you probably can. One way to start is to print out the online version (just in black-and-white) and begin drawing over it with coloured marker pens. Emphasize the areas that mean most to you in your old locality, and those that look attractive in the new one. Pretty soon you'll begin to see what's important to the story, and what can be left out. Take the opportunity to write all over this trial map as well – it's likely you'll trigger ideas for a whole new view of the move. Whether you redraw or simply reuse the maps you acquire, start thinking about the sequence of pages from the audience's point of view. You can zoom in or out, and shoot off down some interesting side streets and design alleys to vary the pace. If the move didn't go exactly to plan, include the disastrous diversions as well. Show, as here, a close-up view of your new area superimposed on a small-scale general map of the whole region.

Now let's start making the online neighbourhood your own! In your image-editing program (if it provides web-linking functions) or web design program, you could add 'hot spots' to your final map, with links to more detailed maps or photos on a new web page, or to interior shots of the rooms in your house. Alternatively, place a link under a map reference – such as Seascale in the map, *opposite* – which takes you to a zoomed-in view, or to some local history text.

SEASCALE

DESIRABLE RESIDENCES

Look for landmarks. You may not pass Big Ben or the Angel of the North on your trip, but there must be a notable sight somewhere in the region! As well as the vital shots of the homes at either end of the moving route, why not include some others along the way? You might, if you're very cunning, even use these impressive pictures to keep your audience guessing exactly which of these palatial dwellings is the final destination. You may be lucky and find your view unobstructed by vehicles and ugly utility poles; if not, you can extend your retouching skills by copying a bush or tree from another shot, and pasting it over the offending item (see page 81).

Butler Required

Can this be the one? A lofty lobby with chandelier would be delightful. Or maybe you're more of a Modernist.

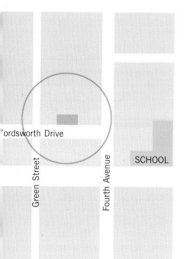

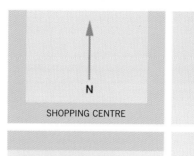

N

SHOPPING CENTRE

'ordsworth Drive

Green Street

Fourth Avenue

SCHOOL

Egremont Street

GOLF COURSE

A LITTLE LOCAL COLOUR

The old conventions: water is blue; grass is green; built-up areas are vaguely brown; these serve well enough for regular maps. Why not make yours different? Why not make your house stand out in bright red? Your street in flaming yellow? Whatever you choose, keep it light and bright so that superimposed text can be easily read.

Using Layers

You can achieve the illusion of depth even with a simple image-editing program. Using a shadow under the coastline kicks it into relief. Try various treatments for the street map – this version has them cut out as white channels, but you could simply edge them with a darker colour for greater contrast.

Decorator Required

Is this Xanadu? Maybe all that white paintwork will prove a problem. Didn't Madonna live here once?

Gardener Required

How to keep all those cars off the lawn? Disagreements might follow...

Lighthouse Keeper Required

Round rugs in the baronial tower? This could be journey's end. I see no ships!

Here are some more images that you can add to your map, whether it's destined for print, email, CD, or the web. Welcome to the extraordinary world of clip-art. Again, you can use these to embellish a printed page or a simple emailed document (perhaps saved as a PDF or as a web page), or you could use them to hide links to other, related web pages in an interactive project. Clip-art has a long history going back to the colourful fragments that children used to paste into scrapbooks a century ago. Then the clippings came free with soap or chocolate bars, now they come in their millions on CDs and on the Internet. The best CD collections prove to be very useful resources for those of us who can't draw; the worst make excellent coasters. There's no reason in any case for you to rely on the commercial product. You have the tools to make your own, far more interesting and personal collection. Flick through your old print albums looking for standout figures, pictures with signboards and posts, perhaps. All these, and many like them, can, with a little scanning, invention and trickery, be made into a useful treasury of instant humour to jazz up your project.

In this particular project, what's needed is direction, in every sense of the word. Pointers, arrows, and signposts for a start. Follow on with street signs (and don't neglect your friendly local speed cameras!) Once you've planted pictures on your map, they need to be tied to their locations with arrows or lines. Here we've drawn circles around the key spots, but the choice is yours. In an image-editing program it's easy to select a circular area, maybe soften the edges of the selection, and change the colour to contrast with the background. You could even leave the small circular selections in colour, and everything else in black and white.

SEASCALE

USING CLIP-ART
Once you have one bit of art, you can easily multiply it. One clip-art door key (or why not scan your own?) can soon become a whole drawer of 'hardware'. Use them as decorative borders or backgrounds, along with squadrons of arrows. And don't forget the old favourites – the endlessly cheerful salesman and the impossibly elegant pointing hand.

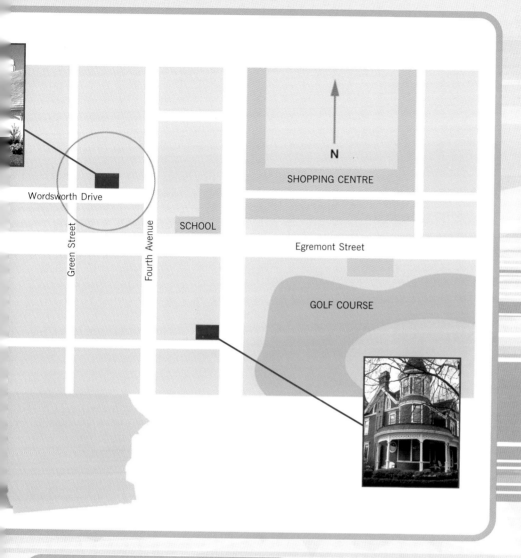

Wordsworth Drive

Green Street

Fourth Avenue

N

SHOPPING CENTRE

SCHOOL

Egremont Street

GOLF COURSE

PICTURE RESOLUTION

When you start adding pictures, don't forget about resolution (see page 14). For a web page, what you see is what the audience will get, so if you've resized your pics to the area you want and they look fine, they are fine. But if you're planning to print your work – as an invitation to that long-promised housewarming party, for example – your images will need to be at about 300dpi. The same applies to the map itself: you must set up your blank canvas at 300dpi at the size you plan to print it, and if it's A4, that means a pretty big file. Alternatively, create it using a drawing or desktop publishing program – their 'vector' graphics can be scaled to any size.

It's easy to develop your opening page into a linked series. Using Word, you can follow the *Web Page Wizard* (accessed via *File>New>General Templates>Web Pages*) or strike out on your own with *View* set to *Web Layout*. To get started, put a page together with some sample text, a couple of pictures (just hit *Insert>Picture>From File* to use some of your own) and maybe a coloured background. Save this page as 'Index', and be sure to save it in *Web Page* format, giving it the '.htm' suffix. Save it again as 'Page 1'. You can now change the elements on this second page while preserving the style of the first, and begin to create links between them.

For example, type 'Next page' at the foot of your 'Index' page, highlight those words, and choose *Hyperlink* from the *Insert* menu. You'll see a dialog box that prompts you to locate 'Index' in your folder. Select the correct file, then view the results with *Web Page Preview* on the *File* menu. Repeat the operation for 'Page 1', inserting something like 'Back to first page' as the text. Now you can rock back and forth between the two. If you have a dedicated web design program, the procedure is similar – see the software's instruction booklet for specific details. You can turn graphics into hyperlinks as well, or draw 'buttons' in an image-editing program and add links and rollovers (see page 148) to those. You can use the *Table* function to organize your words, pictures, and graphics into manageable groups.

Now we're on the finishing straight. Experiment in your image editor to get an idea of what might work as a background. You might choose to stick with one dominant colour, or to assemble a set of contrasting or matching colours. Select a typeface (font) that looks elegant and legible. If you're stuck for choice, try *www.1001freefonts.com* for free ones, *www.myfonts.com* for cheap ones, or *www.fonts.com* for professional ones.

The Grigson

SEASCALE, HERE WE COME!

So much more arresting than the usual moving card – more personal, colourful, versatile, informative, and in every way more fun. Why doesn't everyone do this? Vivid graphics, maps that seem to pop out of the screen, zooming changes of scale, buttons to push, all topped off with an enticing invitation to your new home. Great stuff, and easy to do.

BE KIND TO MODEMS

Way back in this book we spoke about download speeds and file sizes. Now is when all those figures start to mean something! Your image-editing or web-design program will help you get it right. Let's review the basics. More colours or large images means bigger files. Bigger files take longer to download and display. Longer download and display times make for grouchy audiences. The two weapons at your disposal are GIF and JPEG: the first is good at squashing down images with reasonably large areas of flat color, the second works best on photographs (or similar images). PNG is another format for web graphics, but isn't so universally recognized. TIFF is the best format for print, since images can be compressed – though not as much as with JPEG – without losing quality.

How do I burn a CD?
See page 90

are moving...

Arrows of Outrageous Fortune?

All the madness of moving house,
symbolized by a swarm of arrows. Try
setting up a link on the solitary one
to take your visitor to the next page.

Home has Moved Away

The key is in the door, the
drinks are on ice, and all's
well in Wordsworth Drive.

47 WORDSWORTH DRIVE.
Housewarming Party July 8th!

Small office,
Home office...

Now let's explore the possibilities of using your newly acquired skills in the context of a small or home-based business. Most big businesses use sophisticated presentation software and equipment. But if you're thinking of setting up your own business at home, or already have one and want to use your computer to reach out to a wider client base, your digital scrapbooking skills could be used to enhance presentations and win yourself new business. We've used the example of an independent accountant: the type of business that can be run from home, but still have customers that demand professionalism. Of course, the principles can be applied to whatever plans you have in mind!

You may already be aware of the PowerPoint presentation software that comes with Microsoft Office, or Apple's Keynote. These programs start from the premise of creating slideshows, although the results are now more usually displayed as a sequence of images on a computer monitor. PowerPoint offers beginners a helping hand with its crew of *Assistants*, or *Wizards*. For example, there's the *AutoContent*

ESTABLISHING A STYLE

Here we've imagined an accountancy company with an existing 'corporate identity' (the brand and the logo that people come to associate with a company). If you don't already have a logo like your corporate peers, why not design one using your graphics program? A 'vector' drawing or desktop publishing program is ideal, as your logo will scale to any size, but an image editor will give you more scope for cool effects, as long as you work at a high resolution. The colour and type should set the style for all your publicity material, websites and presentations. It needn't be too serious – try something bright and cheerful.

MBP Accountants Online

PRESENTATION

Which Style is Right for You?

Assemble a few ideas and play around with them to see what works.

If you're stuck for illustrative material, you'll find there are numerous

searchable archives of images you can buy, or sometimes use for free.

Wizard, a template slideshow that you can amend with your own words and images. It's easy, and with a bit of perseverance it's also fun.

If you don't have PowerPoint, you can create slideshows using many of the latest image-editing and organizing programs, including Photoshop Elements and Apple iPhoto – and they can look equally professional. Just watch out for the amount of control you'll have over playback. For example, your slideshow may be saved as a movie file. That's fine if you want your audience to watch passively as it plays through, but when you're presenting 'live' you'll want to be able to move between slides as and when you choose. It's best to make a self-playing presentation file that runs under its own steam and lets you click to move it along.

You can approach this type of project in the same way as you plan your family album. Ask yourself: who is the intended audience? Is this a presentation to establish your credentials, or has it got a specific message? Sketch out the main points on paper and push them around until you see a structure emerging. Does the presentation need to be simple and colourful, or sophisticated and modern? We've done both.

Following the basic slideshow format, you can build in the capability to move forward or back, or skip, but the presentation will essentially be linear. If your software supports interactivity, different possibilities arise. You could offer two pathways through the show: one giving a flavour of the business, the other detailing your proposals or business plan. This will give viewers a richer experience, but it's up to you to make sure they

MBP Accoun

Opening the do to financial secu

- Flexible
- Responsive
- Experienced
- Trustworthy

Images and Words
Balance words and images for maximum effect. Less than 20 words suffice for this opener, combined with a striking and inviting graphic. Strong colours and uniform type treatment hold the whole screen together.

Leave Nothing Out
Setting up the office shot is vital. The message is: we have the technology and a relaxed working environment. Ergo, we can do good work for you – and will be pleased to hear from you. But couldn't we do something more imaginative with images like this? See page 74!

WHERE'S THE ARTWORK?
Why not scan your existing business documents and use the image as a background for each slide, or turn any flat, scannable object you can find around your desk into a graphic you can reuse on every slide? Alternatively, why not do what we've done here and take some photos of your home office? For those all-important facts and figures, you can easily make graphs and charts in PowerPoint, or you can import them from Excel or another spreadsheet program. If you've got Microsoft's Office suite (or an alternative) installed, all the software you need is right there on your machine already! If you want to put something together really quickly, PowerPoint comes with its own clip-art library containing thousands of items, which you can even search: just tap in 'success', for example, and your reward is images of trophies, rosettes, and leaping figures. And it's not just images – there are movie clips and sound files as well. You can find plenty more clip-art online, but the best quality at reasonable prices comes with CD- or DVD-based collections such as Hemera BizArt (www.hemera.com).

Show the Detail

It's not all technology. There are still people here with conventional diaries and a serious attitude. Our studious man at work here is actually 'tele-working' from his local restaurant. Does he *never* stop work? Find out what more you can do with images like this on page 74!

nts Online

Image courtesy of Hewlett-Packard

don't get lost! *Forward/Back/Home* commands are standard, and even better is a navigation system that appears on each screen – rather like a website. In fact, an increasingly popular way to create presentations is to make a website and store it on the computer you're presenting with, or deliver it on a CD-R. With a few extra clicks you can put it online too.

Now it's time to start our introductory sequence. Our first, bold and colourful version uses an 'open door' clip-art graphic. In PowerPoint, draw a picture box, then go to *Insert>Picture>Clip* and find this image in the collection supplied. Of course, you'll also want to use your own images, and you can import these using *Insert>Picture>From File*.

Our graphic gives way to the draft company logo in the second slide. The animated 'transition' between the slides is programmed in the *SlideShow* menu, which offers dozens of different transition styles, as well as a *Random* setting to cycle through them all. The simplest choices are a straight 'cut' or a dissolve, but, whichever you choose, resist the temptation to use more than two or three styles in one presentation.

The screen shown *right* is genuinely a 'work in progress'. We're trying out several versions of the company name and logo to see which works

OUR WORK IN PROGRESS: CREATING THE LOGO

Effects like bevelling, embossing and soft shadows, now standard in graphics programs, can help turn an ordinary piece of type into a logo. Don't forget the importance of hierarchy: make the most important element the biggest, so it catches the eye first, then fit the rest in smaller type to underline it. You may not need to use an image or pictogram if you can make the type strong enough.

ccountants Online
ccountants Online

- Flexible
- Responsive
- Experienced
- Trustworthy

nds

e door

security

MBP
ACCOUNTANTS

best (remember a logo often works better as a label than as a title). You can design everything within your presentation software or create graphics in your image-editing program, then import it. The flexibility of programs like this is there to be exploited, especially when it comes to the colour and style of text and backgrounds. Embossing and shadows are easily produced in PowerPoint's *Font* menu, while other graphics software can be used for more complex effects. Always have the viewer's eyesight – and the limited resolution of the screen – in mind: avoid typefaces with fine strokes, and fancy script styles, and take care with colour combinations. Colours on the monitor can be as vibrant as you like, but the effect over several screens could frazzle sensitive eyeballs.

Next, for our first presentation, we've added some pictures of our (unusually tidy) office. Got the digital camera ready? Take your shots and import them into PowerPoint as before. Designing your slides gets all the trickier with photos to fit in, so try a fairly regular layout with one picture per screen and perhaps your logo staying in the same place. Charts and graphs, which you can create in any spreadsheet, will help to present complex information and add to the gravitas of the presentation, as long as you keep them simple and legible. Once all your elements are decided on, you can play around and get the slides looking right.

This is a good time to consider that you needn't build your presentation from the ground up using PowerPoint or Keynote. Have a look at our second presentation on pages 74 and 75. You could use any word processing or image-editing program to produce these images. Import them into your presentation or slideshow program, and just use it as a 'slide projector' to string together your ready-made screens.

Let's try this process in Photoshop Elements. The sequence of operations could go as follows: make a new document 512 pixels wide

MBP Accountan

Your business—safe in our hands

- ○ **Flexible**
- ○ Responsive
- ○ Experienced
- ○ Trustworthy

GETTING DOWN TO BUSINESS

Having imported some more images and thought out the structure of your presentation, you can start to create a progression of slides. Elements such as the 'bullet points' above can be made to appear successively, fading in or flipping on like a light. To make sure your audience follows what's going on, you could highlight them successively in the opening slide of each section of your show. By copying each slide from the last, or using a master slide, you can keep everything consistent, so that items transition naturally from one slide to the next rather than jumping around confusingly.

How do I add music and video to a slideshow?
See page 94

LIES, DAMNED LIES. . . AND STATISTICS

Check out a few companies' graphs and charts. It's surprising how many of them don't show a full scale rising from zero on the upward axis. Although the cause might be space-saving, focusing on a narrow band of figures usually has the effect of accentuating small, upward fluctuations (in other words, it makes a small amount of growth look huge). If the statistics are not so good, a lot of companies create graphs that show them as small blips in a longer timeframe.

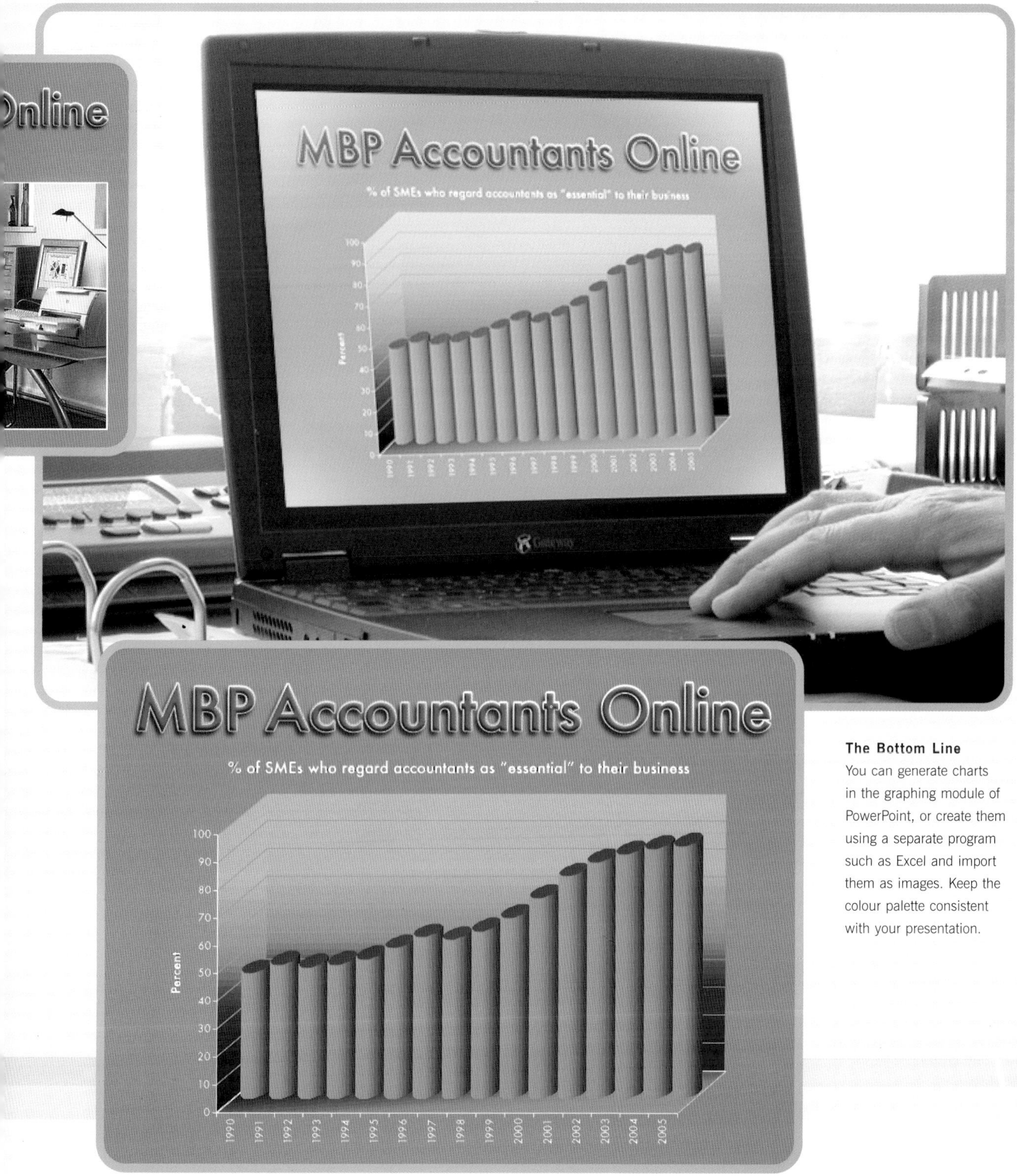

MBP Accountants Online
% of SMEs who regard accountants as "essential" to their business
Percent
100
90
80
70
60
50
40
30
20
10
0
1990
1991
1992
1993
1994
1995
1996
1997
1998
1999
2000
2001
2002
2003
2004
2005

The Bottom Line

You can generate charts in the graphing module of PowerPoint, or create them using a separate program such as Excel and import them as images. Keep the colour palette consistent with your presentation.

CROPS, DETAILS, EFFECTS: OUR SECOND PRESENTATION

We think you'll agree this is much more like it: it's much simpler, much snappier, a touch more sophisticated – and far easier to do! Simply take a few pictures from interesting angles, or use your eagle eye to select the most interesting details to home in on and crop. We've used our man at work shot, then applied a Posterize effect to it. While you can do this in Photoshop Elements (Image>Adjust>Posterize), for example, we achieved this effect in a page layout program by changing the contrast (including the contrast between the colours). This creates an image we can use as a background. We've then added some other cropped pictures, and added some text on top. Simplicity itself!

by 342 pixels high (an ideal slide format, as it'll display on any system); produce your artwork and type as required; save the results as a series of TIFF files; and import these into PowerPoint, Elements' own Create Slide Show feature, or your preferred alternative. Photoshop Elements' 'layers' let you move and scale graphical elements independently, and you can use the *File, Duplicate* command to make a copy of your first slide, complete with layers, as a separate file to start your second. The same approach can be used with any software capable of producing image files – Paint Shop Pro, CorelDRAW, DrawPlus, or even a desktop publishing program.

Whichever style you decide on, the results can be incorporated into a website, sent out by email, burned onto CD, or printed out on paper, overhead projector transparencies – or even slides! Alternatively, turn the whole idea on its head, give your presentation software a day off from the office, and use it to make a slideshow of your latest family snaps.

Opening the door
to financial security

RESIZING POWERPOINT
FOR REGULAR PRINT

Choose Web Content in the PowerPoint Preferences dialog, and select Picture. Choose one of the two large monitor options, 1800 x 1440 pixels, for example. This is also a good setting for video projection. When you save the show, also save a copy as JPEG files. You'll get a folder full of individual files which your conventional printer can reinterpret as smaller, but higher-resolution images.

Wedding bells: online or video

If any event is guaranteed to get the photographer snapping and the video camera out of hibernation, it's a wedding. The unique combination of setting, colour, and emotion make for powerful images. But isn't it unfortunate that all too often such a momentous event is left to languish in a rarely viewed album, or on an anonymous videotape? So why not make your wedding photography – whether still, video, or both – something to remember? Over the next few pages we'll look at raising your photography above the rest, and how you can share the fruits of your efforts on videotape, CD, and the Web. The starting point of the project is, of course, the event itself. If you've been asked to photograph a wedding, make sure you go well equipped. A digital camera and/or video camera are the basics, along with a good solid tripod and microphone. Never rely on the on-camera microphone for your important jobs.

A digital video camera is strongly recommended. Not only does it offer superb picture quality, it's the easiest to transfer to the computer. But don't worry if you've an analogue model – we'll see later that there are ways of importing video from this too. Make sure you take plenty of spares: batteries, tapes, and memory cards. And, although it doesn't deserve to be called a spare, a conventional SLR camera too.

Official Photographs
Official wedding photographs can be clichéd but, used with less formal shots, make an ideal basis for your production. This one was over-zealous with that filter!

Informal Photos
Capture the formalities, of course, but also try and catch the bride and groom looking at their most relaxed, or crop to charming details like this.

WEDDING – OR WARNING – BELLS?

One of the great things about digital video is that it's easy to review. You can perform simple edits on your PC almost immediately. And if you have a well-specified laptop or notebook computer, you could even provide a preview screening during the reception. Take your notebook computer and you could even set up a webcam for those relatives unable to attend! But don't forget the smaller details: remember those spare batteries! Digital cameras and camcorders have a voracious appetite for power, rather like the best man. It's also a good idea to ensure that all batteries are fully charged, and to pack the relevant AC adaptors too – especially handy when filming at the reception.

Group Photographs

Producing a set of group photographs is more or less obligatory for the official photographer. Photos of large groups, such as the one shown here, are an ideal way of ensuring that as many guests as possible are included in your production, including those who might not make their way to the reception. But getting everyone to keep their eyes open is another matter, lady in the white hat!

Spontaneous Shots

More so than official photos, spontaneous shots often capture the true atmosphere of the day. Don't worry if such photos are not perfect (they rarely are), you can always improve them digitally, as we'll explore in this project.

The Dance Floor

Like spontaneous photos, video of people dancing (or socializing generally) often provides some of the best memories of the reception. Video footage of family members dancing self-consciously is particularly prized, of course.

When photographing a wedding, take a leaf from the book of the professional photographer and work to a checklist. This is easy enough to compile and should include all the principal stages of the event. This way you'll always ensure that you're at the right place at the right time, and that you haven't missed anything crucial. And, like the professional, you shouldn't skimp on the number of photos (or the amount of video footage) that you take. It's both easy and desirable to cut down the amount of material later, but it's impossible to recreate any parts that you missed. More digital data costs little or no extra, so there's no excuse.

If you're not allowed to video the service itself, use your video camera to record the sound. Few venues will have any objections to this. When you come to compile the movie, you can insert still images (which may have been taken before, during, or after the service) to provide the visuals. The audio track alone will be sufficient to trigger memories, while the stills will make up for the lack of 'live' video. Prepare yourself for this by taking some 'cutaway' shots – general views of the venue, floral displays, or even waiting guests – either as still or video footage that can be inserted into the 'audio only' passages.

Cutaways are an excellent general-purpose resource. Not only can they be used to fill in sound-only passages, you can use them to link scenes, provide transitions, and even – when converted to still images – as titles on a web page. You could also do the reverse, and create material – such as backgrounds and title shots – from still images. Often only a little manipulation is required (such as recropping or removing backgrounds, as *opposite*, where we've picked out the bouquet).

WHAT TO DO ON A RECONNAISSANCE MISSION

If you have been commissioned to take photographs or video at a wedding (whether as the official photographer or not) it makes very good sense to visit the venue (or venues) in advance to determine the best places to take shots from. You should also take the opportunity to discuss your intentions with representatives of the venues. In some churches, for example, you may find that still photography is permitted during the service but video photography is not. In others, no photography whatsoever is allowed during the more solemn parts. Respect whatever rules are in force. If they seem to preclude recording important parts of the ceremony, don't worry; with a little skill and digital sleight of hand during the editing we can make good any omissions.

CATCHING THE BOUQUET

It's very useful to collect shots that can be used as titles on a website or video or to separate sections of your project into 'chapters'. When these have not been recorded during the event, it's easy to produce them from some of the other photographs you've collected. Here's a good case in point. The bride's bouquet, shown clearly in this group photo, makes an ideal detail to catch! The final image has a variety of uses: a 'thank you' card, perhaps; a page in your scrapbook; or a web page background.

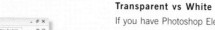

Transparent vs White

If you have Photoshop Elements version 3 or higher, you'll find that when you first click with the *Background Eraser* your 'Background' layer changes to 'Layer 0', and areas you erase become transparent (shown as a checkerboard). With older versions, it will erase to white. Before adding a new background, use the *Magic Wand* to select the white area, then press the Delete key to clear it, leaving it transparent.

Removing the Background

Begin by importing the image into your image-editing application and zoom in on the bouquet. As you only require this part of the photo, crop the image reasonably tightly around it. Removing the background is a task for the kinds of tools discussed on page 51, and once again the *Background Eraser* in Photoshop Elements is a particularly good option. The *Lasso* or *Magic Wand* tools could be used in other programs.

Adding a New Background

Once the original background is transparent, you can add a new one, either by pasting in a different image or by creating a new layer and filling it. Drag the new layer to the bottom in the *Layers* palette. Here we've used the *Gradient* tool to blend between two colours. Notice how our chosen colours complement those of the bouquet.

When we look back at important events such as a wedding, we usually have a romanticized view. The weather was perfect (even if there was actually a howling gale), everyone was happy, and the setting was like a dream. But reviewing the photographs we are quickly reminded of the reality. Things were not entirely as we remembered! But with a little post-production work we can improve on that reality and put right many of the problems that are all too obvious in the photos.

The image-enhancement techniques we use in such circumstances fall into two broad camps. In one there are the corrective measures. These amount to manipulating those photographs that have minor faults, such as being a little dull (underexposed), bright (overexposed), or otherwise suffering faults affecting the whole image. In most cases, these can easily be corrected, often using quick-fix commands such as *Auto Enhance* or *Auto Correct* (see pages 140 to 143).

In the other are those photos that are substantially perfect, but are in some minor way compromised. The photo, *right*, is a good example. The photographer has successfully 'caught the moment' and recorded the intimate and memorable moment of the couple's kiss. Sadly, at this precise moment another guest has strolled by. Although the photo is still great, it would be much better if this person was removed from the scene so that the couple were truly the centre of attention.

Fortunately we have the *Clone* (*Rubber Stamp* in Photoshop and Photoshop Elements) and *Healing Brush* tools, which enable the removal of the errant guest. Rather than removing superfluous detail by using tools like the background eraser, the *Clone* tool lets us cover up distractions by cloning – copying – other parts of the scene. It's a very powerful and versatile tool. You could also use it to clone material into the scene. For example, were one of the guests in a group photo to have blinked during the shot (and how often has this happened to you?) we could clone their open eyes from another shot into this image.

Some people find making overt changes such as these a little alarming. Wedding photographs are meant to be a record of the day's events and those events should be authentic. Most of us, though, want our wedding photographs to be as near perfect as possible. With your combined collections of official photographs, and those of guests, you have a wealth of material to choose from. And you could include a mix of 'perfect' images (using image editing techniques) and those that show a more authentic picture of the day's events.

Clone, Rubber Stamp, and Healing Tools
Clone tools are best described as painting tools. But, unlike other painting tools that use a solid colour, they copy parts of the image, such as foliage here, and paint them to another.

Random Cloning
It is important that you select different 'clone from' points when covering a large subject such as this. This creates a natural and random result, and avoids making the fix look too obvious. Pay particular attention to the boundary between cloned and original material.

REMOVING A DISTRACTION!

Removing an unwanted element from a scene is an ideal use for the Clone tool. Here we'll use it to remove the guest who has innocently walked by at the precise moment that the photographer, concentrating on the bride and groom, took the photo. The photo itself is otherwise perfect and, even with the guest in shot, would make an excellent print. But notice how our corrected photo (bottom) is compositionally much more powerful.

The Finished Portrait

How did we make the unwanted interloper (*top left*) quit the scene (*above*)? It's all thanks to our image-editing software (*top right*). The professionals use these tricks too, you know.

Those ad hoc photos taken at the reception, whether by you or other guests, often need a little more remedial action to make them look good. This is not necessarily because guests have poor photographic skills (mixtures of alcohol and emotion can compromise those skills!), but rather because the situations in which these photographs have been taken are not conducive to good results. Guests will, in general, be using compact cameras (whether digital or conventional), and will be aiming to make their own, informal record of the day.

Fortunately, most cameras today are capable of very good results, even when used in fully automatic mode. Hence many of the exposure problems that plagued earlier generations are gone. With small, but surprisingly powerful, flash units, photography in the dimly lit conditions of the reception are a cinch. But wait: flash brings its own problems. If you watch professional photographers in such situations you'll see that they tend to use a reflector, or flash units that are either mounted away from the camera, or angled upward to the ceiling. These lighting techniques give softer, less shadowed lighting that is more flattering to the subject. They also avoid two problems common to on-camera flash units: redeye and hotspots.

Redeye is a result of using a flash unit that is very close to the camera lens, hence the glowing eyes. Hotspots have a similar root cause. This time the light from the flash unit reflects strongly from the centre of the scene (such as from a shiny wall in the background), producing lighting that is very uneven across the scene. Fortunately, both hotspots and redeye are easy to fix digitally.

The simplest way to remove this hotspot is to select the back wall and then replace it with a uniform colour, based on the original. Use the *Lasso* to draw around the perimeter of the wall, with the selection boundary close to the subjects.

REDEYE

This photo shows where the power and direction of the flash has illuminated the blood vessels at the back of the subject's eyes. Many image-editing applications (such as Photoshop Elements, here) are equipped with redeye removal tools.

Select the *Redeye Removal* tool and use a brush size similar to that of the pupil.

With only the wall selected, use the *Eyedropper* tool to sample the colour of the wall away from the hotspot (over the bride's shoulder, for example). Use this colour to paint over the selection. In the finished print there is no sign of the hotspot, yet the colour remains authentic. A quick fix that won't be obvious.

By brushing over the pupil with the *Redeye Removal* tool the red glow is replaced with a more authentic dark grey. Notice that only the red has been replaced; the small white highlight – the twinkle – in the eye remains.

COOLING DOWN THE HOTSPOTS

The direct flash light has here reflected off the wall behind the couple, resulting in a bright and unsightly patch – a hotspot. Removing it will emphasize the subjects of the photo.

Once you've collected and, where appropriate, manipulated your images of the wedding, you can set about building a web page. As we've already explored, there are many proprietary applications designed for webpage – and website – building, but many image-editing applications also contain the tools for building simple gallery sites. Pages are usually based on a limited range of templates, but you may be able to customize them using basic tools similar to those found in desktop publishing applications. This way you can lay your pages out exactly as you wish them to appear on-screen. Once again, remember that any photographic images destined for web use need to be saved in JPEG format, compressed to make them as small as possible without losing too much quality. Have a look back at page 44 to remind yourself about the pros and cons of JPEG compression and the importance of previewing how your image will turn out.

Video-editing applications, including popular products such as Apple's iMovie, Windows Movie Maker and Roxio's VideoWave, provide the option of exporting very heavily compressed video footage to files small enough to be made available for download from a website. While the quality of such material is not great, a short clip can be ideal for enlivening your site. Ten or 15 seconds – perhaps of confetti being thrown at the church door – is perfect.

THE WEDDING WEB PAGE
Web-design software provides the tools to create web pages that are as simple or as complex as you wish. It's a good idea, particularly if there are a lot of photographs, to provide a front page that offers fast and direct access to a particular section. And don't place too many photos on a single page. Images, even when optimized for the web, will download slowly, and you don't want modem users to give up in despair while waiting!

---

wedding.htm

See the wedding photos here

Create Hyperlink

URL: http://www.johnandsarah.com/wedding/photos.htm

Bookmark:

Target: _self

Tooltip:

Access key:

☑ Open in new window   Options...

Clear Link   OK   Cancel

Edit / Edit & HTML / HTML / Preview /

John and Sarah's Wedding

www.ourweddingsite.co.uk

Apple   .Mac   Amazon   eBay   Yahoo!   News ▼   Google UK

Hints and Tips

Web Galleries

Photoshop Elements and other image-editing applications let you create web photo galleries with just a few clicks. Although these are basic (and provide little opportunity for customization), they're ideal for distributing pictures quickly. Such a site can be created in minutes and can give all those unable to attend an event the chance to enjoy the day with minimal delay. All you have to do is tell them the web address (URL) to go to. The more entrepreneurial can also use a web gallery to encourage guests to order reprints of their favourite photos!

Online movies

By applying heavy compression to selected footage, it's quite feasible to post short video clips to the web. Apple's QuickTime format, for example, supports every quality level from quick and dirty' to Hollywood. The complete ceremony will be too demanding for most people's Internet connections, but highlights are easily downloaded and enjoyed – particularly if they include the funniest bits.

Instant website

You can share your photos without any software at all using an online photo printing service such as *www.ofoto.com* or *www.fotango.com*. Upload your photos and add them to your personal online gallery, then email the URL to everyone.

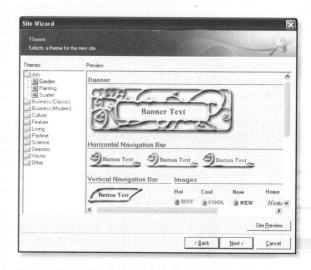

Links are the Thing

As we've mentioned before, it's links that make the web go around. In Namo WebEditor *opposite*, the link creation process is as simple as a click or two. Using the supplied templates *above*, you can set up all your pages' properties, including background and link colours and graphical styles, in one go.

Hold the Front Page!

Here's an ideal front page for a website. A simple, uncluttered design makes it obvious what links have been provided. By clicking on the appropriate icon, visitors to the website can open separate photo galleries – including the bride and groom, bridesmaids, and friends and family. On this site an additional button starts the (appropriately compressed) video.

John and Sarah's Wedding

The Bride and Groom

The Bridesmaids

Friends and Relations

August 7th 2002

The Video

Editing the movie footage is probably simpler than editing the still images – so don't panic! Assuming you've used a digital video camera, you need only hook up the camera to the computer using a FireWire cable (called iLink by Sony) and start the software.

Applications such as the Mac-based iMovie (*shown here*) have made video editing simple. The software takes control of your camera and will download your chosen footage from tape. Windows has the more basic but useful Movie Maker, and you can buy other low-cost editors such as Adobe Premiere Elements, Roxio VideoWave (*www.roxio.com*) and Ulead Video Studio (*www.ulead.com*). For the heavy hitters there's Adobe Premiere Pro for Windows and Apple's Final Cut on the Mac.

Once the clips have been captured, you can begin creating your own blockbuster. First, drag clips to the 'timeline' in the order you'd like them to appear. At this stage you can delete unwanted footage and trim clips of superfluous material (don't worry – you're only deleting the copy on your computer, the original tape remains unaffected).

When you've got the sequence right you can begin adding transitions. Transitions define the way one scene blends into the next. Normally, one scene cuts straight to the next, but you can fade one into another, fade to black, or choose something more avant-garde!

You can also add titles – and even captions. For the titles you might want to overlay text onto a selected video clip (perhaps a scene-setting shot), or you can import the still images you made earlier as a background. Still images can also be imported and used alongside movie footage, either individually or as a slideshow (see Project Five, page 66).

If you used an analogue video camera, you won't be able to import footage directly into the computer. You'll need an analogue-to-digital converter (such as Dazzle's Hollywood Bridge or Formac's Studio) to convert the video signal into a digital form. The digitized signal can then be imported – and split into clips – as above. See page 145 for more.

Step Aside, Mr Spielberg!

Simple 'drag and drop' technology means digital video editing is now remarkably simple. Drag clips to the timeline in the preferred sequence, then add any effects or transitions required. Click on the *Play* button to watch your masterpiece unfold. iMovie, here, also permits two additional soundtracks to be mixed with the original video to provide background music, or perhaps narration. Once you've assembled your production you can copy the movie back to videotape, to CD, or to a file for the web.

The beauty of using digital video is the quality. You can expect 500-line resolution, substantially more than offered by conventional VHS (around 240), and noticeably more than the so-called 'hi-band' formats (S-VHS and Hi-8), which could only manage 400. And, unlike these formats, whose quality will drop further when edited, digital video loses virtually nothing in terms of quality even when intensively edited.

But there is a cost to this quality. When you download your video footage you'll notice your hard disk space is being consumed at a phenomenal rate. At full quality, one minute's video will require 230 megabytes of disk space. If you've an hour's worth of raw footage from your wedding, you'll need no less than 12 gigabytes of free space to accommodate it. That's not a problem with the 100-plus gigabyte hard drives that are now common, but you do need to watch the space.

Of course, you're unlikely to use all the footage you download. There will be duplicated material, inappropriate footage (taken, for example, when you forgot to press the *Pause* button), and superfluous shots. These can – indeed *must* – be discarded. Your aim in producing your movie is to tell the story of the day's events. If you can do that in 15 minutes rather than 45, so much the better.

There's nothing wrong with using a fairly basic video-editing program – people have made productions using iMovie that have been shown at major film festivals! If you feel the need for something more advanced, Mac users can choose the mid-priced Final Cut Express, while Pinnacle's Liquid Edition for Windows (*www.pinnaclesys.com*) is a little more affordable than the Pro versions of Final Cut or Premiere. Serious professionals will want one of these products plus a special effects package such as Adobe AfterEffects or Pinnacle Commotion.

However you choose to produce your movie, the next question is how to show it. By connecting from your computer to your DVD camera, then on to your VHS machine, you can simply record it onto tape – but it seems a shame to convert crisp digital to fuzzy analogue.

Apple Final Cut Pro

High-end video-editing programs such as Apple's Final Cut Pro allow multiple audio and video tracks to be mixed at will. The degree of control and the number of effects is substantially greater than with entry-level applications, and these packages are used every day by professional editors right up to feature film level.

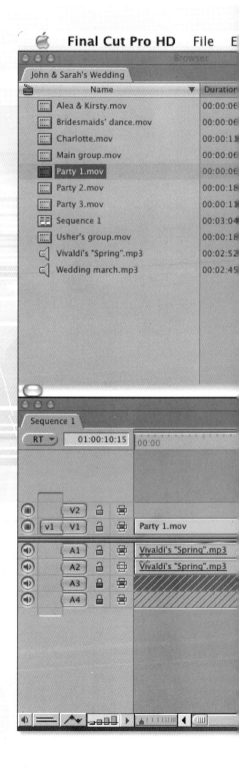

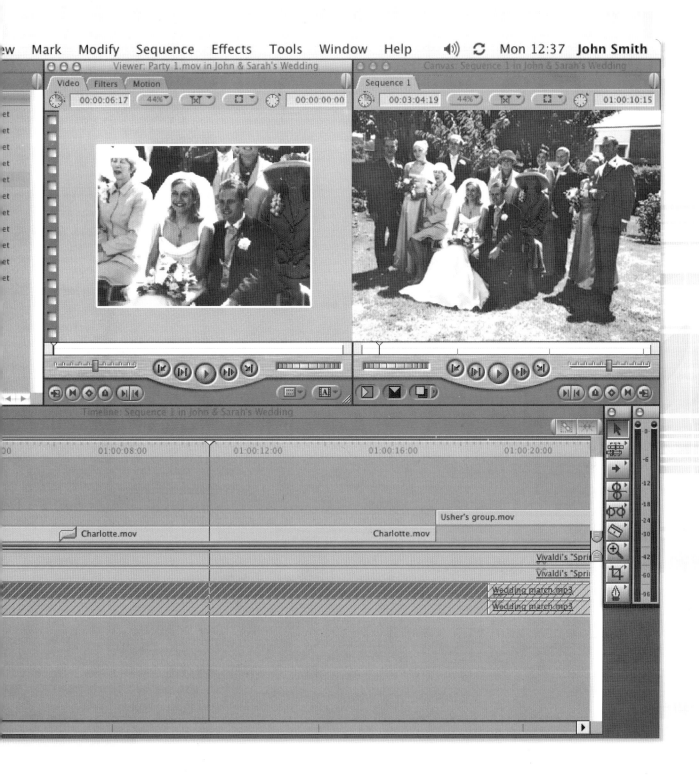

Using CDs as a distribution medium for your production is both viable and economic. A standard CD-R, 'burnt' in your computer's CD recorder drive, can hold a large collection of images and compressed movie footage, which can then be viewed on any computer – although you won't be able to maintain the same quality as the original MiniDV. Using any CD burner program for Windows, you need only drag and drop your folders of images and video onto a window to include them on the CD. Mac users have CD-burning built into their operating system.

You can also use widely available software to record VideoCDs – a common option in slideshow programs. This is a CD-based format, which you can write using a CD recorder drive, but can be played in many DVD players as well as in computer CD-ROM drives. You can store up to one hour's worth of video on a single CD, and although the quality isn't great, it's about as good as VHS.

More and more PCs now come with DVD recorder drives, and if yours didn't, you can add one on for less money that you might think. This enables you to create true DVDs compatible with any DVD player. With appropriate authoring software, such as iDVD on the Mac or one of the various DVD creators for Windows, you can produce a DVD complete with chapters, animated menus, and a dynamic mix of audio, video, and still images! Your wedding DVD, for example, might contain the complete video in its original edited form (and quality) along with high-resolution photo albums and a host of additional material, such as guest lists and other ephemera, for users to view as they wish.

Creating your DVD
Applications like iDVD make DVD production easy. By using simple menu selections and dragging and dropping screen elements, you can make a DVD video that's every bit as impressive as a commercially mastered product.

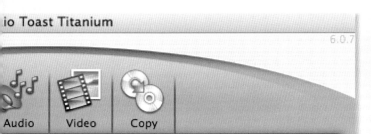

io Toast Titanium

6.0.7

Audio　Video　Copy

2923 items - 327.9 MB ?

327.9 MB

22 K

15.7 MB

25.5 MB

66 K

93.9 MB

13.3 MB

140 K

118.7 MB

22.8 MB

26.4 MB

THE WEDDING CD

Transferring your wedding video and photo collection to CD is simple and makes a very economic way of distributing the production. Talk to the bride and groom – they may commission you to produce one for each member of the family and selected guests as a 'thank you' to them. Use a still for the cover, too!

Burning the CD

Writing files – whether photos, movies, web pages, or text – to a CD is simple using applications such as Roxio's Toast (Mac). Drag selected files to the appropriate window, and press the button. After a few minutes your CD will have been recorded and verified (checked for errors).

Kidz @ play multimedia

After the rather formal and rigid structure of a wedding, a child's birthday party can come as something of a relief. There are no formal photos to take and no shooting script to follow to the letter. But that's not to say that you don't need to do a little forward planning. It's always a good idea to know the what, where and when of events to make sure you don't miss out on the fun. This is particularly important if you've been delegated as photographer, and are not the master of ceremonies!

You'll also be in the fortunate position that most children enjoy being photographed, and will be happy to pose for you – even if that means pulling faces. But you'll also need your skills to cajole those who are more camera shy: they (or at least their parents) will thank you for it afterwards.

It is the blowing out of the birthday candles that represents the high spot of the day, and this is where you could have problems, should you be covering the event with both still and video cameras. This could be the ideal time to appoint an assistant, as trying to operate two cameras simultaneously (and successfully) is impossible. Know your limitations!

Catch the Moment
Painted faces, a touching kiss. Photos that make children's birthday parties so special.

CAUGHT IN THE ACT

A children's entertainer makes for great photography, both still and video. Totally captivated by this balloon modeller, these children are at their most natural. Keeping your distance helps preserve the natural expressions and avoids the audience becoming self-conscious. Remember to vary your position when recording a video: no matter how compelling the performance the video will become tedious if it is all recorded as one continuous shot from one angle.

It's a Date

Add a simple title to the combined image and – most important – give the production a date! *Layer Effects* in Elements have been used here too, firstly to give the original image a glow (called an *Outer Glow* effect), and to give the text a *Bevel* appearance.

The Original Photo

The photo of the birthday boy blowing out the candle on the cake will make an ideal centrepiece for our cover, or for your scrapbook. We'll use the *Elliptical Marquee* in Photoshop Elements to select an oval vignette that we can paste onto a background of jelly beans!

MAKING A CD COVER

Memorable events call for memorable photos. You can use the photos you take on the day not only to create an album that can be stored on a CD, but to illustrate the CD box. Many image-editing applications include templates for CD covers that make getting the size right simple. You can also print labels for the CD itself – or some inkjets can even print directly onto the CD. Why not get the birthday boy or girl to draw the picture?

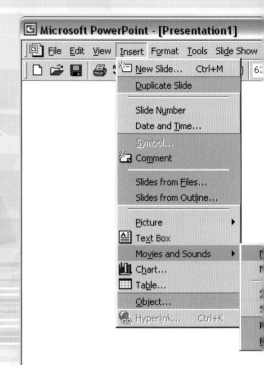

Whether you're using still or video cameras, don't forget that there's more to a birthday than just a party. You can photograph the child waking in the morning (usually very early!) and exploring for presents. And, at the end of the day, heading off to bed proud to be a year older, if not wiser. For moviemaking especially, these additional scenes help better tell the story of the day and really are appreciated in later years.

The idea of putting images onto CD is a good one. Despite the tendency to get scratched if mishandled or stored poorly, they have proved to be a very robust storage medium, and one that (despite the high price of pre-recorded CDs!) is very economical. They also have the advantage of being compatible with just about every contemporary computer, no matter what the flavour of operating system.

It is also a very simple matter to copy a large number of image files to a CD. This gives anyone who has a copy of the disk a chance to view, and even print the images. But a directory full of images is not the best of presentation styles. No, wouldn't it be better if we presented the album of images as a slideshow, and even set that slideshow to music?

As we mentioned in Project Five, you'll find that many image-editing and organizing applications will generate slideshows for you, while presentation programs like PowerPoint and Keynote provide even more possibilities for formatting and interactivity. Once you've created a slideshow, you can usually export a 'standalone' copy that can be written to CD and will replay itself on someone else's computer without needing any other software. In some cases you may need to create separate versions for Mac and Windows users.

When you create the slideshow, you can determine how long each shot appears on screen (five seconds is typical), and introduce transitions, again as in Project Five, to make the change from one image to the next more interesting and less abrupt. You can choose from a wide variety of transitions, ranging from a gentle fade through to the wacky (and occasionally disturbing) mosaics and explosions. Like most way-out effects, extreme transitions are rarely appropriate, but once in a while they can be a fun way to grab attention.

Before burning your production onto CDs or posting it on a website, you can add some music. A good soundtrack can really 'make' your show, and there's no doubt it will make it more enjoyable to watch. You can arrange the sound clips to line up with the on-screen action, and fade smoothly in and out between one piece of audio and the next.

Don't worry if your image editor doesn't offer slideshows. If Microsoft Office is on your PC, you have a copy of PowerPoint, which is more than capable of producing good-looking slideshows with music and even video clips. Alternatively, treat yourself to one of the many cheap slideshow programs for Windows. On the Mac, iPhoto has a slideshow builder.

Let's Put on the Show Right Here
Creating a slideshow involves selecting a sequence of photos, placing transitions between the individual images, and adding some background music. The creation process often involves dragging and dropping images into a chosen sequence, then dropping a transitional effect between. After you've added your choice of music, your show is ready for burning to CD, or posting on the web.

MUSIC TO YOUR EARS

The choice of musical soundtrack for your slideshow can be a big problem. Your first choice will probably be to use something appropriate, such as your child's favourites, or even a collection of party songs. The problem with most commercially produced music is that it is protected by copyright, and you shouldn't include it in your own productions without permission, although it'll rarely cause problems if the video is purely for family consumption. Similar restrictions apply to your own recordings of live performers, including the organist, choir or other musicians at a wedding – an extra video fee may be payable to cover this.

Fortunately, there are plenty of alternatives. You'll find that there are extensive collections of music available on CD that are variously described as 'copyright free' or 'royalty free', meaning that once you've bought the CD you're allowed to use the tracks in whatever way you like (definitely not true of ordinary music CDs!) There may still be some restrictions, so check the reproduction licence details before you buy. Otherwise, why not create your own background music – or better still, get your children to do it!

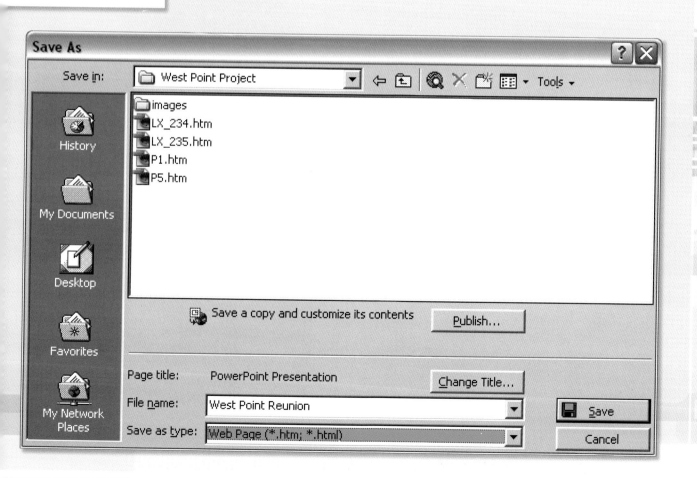

Bear necessities: record a collection

Whether our passion is model trains, cars, antiquarian books, or, as here, rare or antique toys, we all seem to have an insatiable desire to collect things. And, if we're successful, our collections run the risk of growing out of control! Digital technology gives you a whole new way of displaying your collection – and, if it is valuable in monetary terms, also of tracking your assets and maintaining effective records. So don't get lost in the woods!

The first step is an accurate photographic record. Isn't your collection photogenic? So wouldn't a photographic archive make an attractive addition to your collection? As we explored in the introduction to this book, the Internet gives you a unique and unparalleled opportunity to talk to other collectors, sharing your passions with like-minded individuals. With digital scrapbooking techniques, you can build a website, advertise your interest in acquiring new items, email pictures, or put together a CD – not to mention a traditional paper scrapbook.

This project will show you how to record the unique features of your pride and joy. An overall view makes a good opening page, but you'll need to record each item too, including its 'pedigree', such as a maker's marque, hallmark, or – as in this collection – label, such as Steiff.

Bearing your All!

The simplest of photo records of a collection would involve nothing more than arranging them on the floor and taking a quick snap. But this hardly does justice to you, your passion, or your collection. Think of all the effort (and probably money) that has gone into building it and, by spending only a little more time, you can display your collection to better advantage. Show off the unique details of each item that makes it appealing, unique, or valuable. This will provide the source material for an interactive web page. See page 109 for our finished example!

THE IMPORTANCE OF PENCIL AND PAD

We all seem to hate spending time – or wasting time, as we sometimes see it – planning. Whether our project is straightforward or complex, many of us like plunging straight in at the deep end. It's the same when we buy a new camera or computer, but fail to take time out to read the instructions. Only later do we discover that, had we done so, we would have found our new tool to be easier to use and far more powerful than we'd realized. So, spend just a little time noting down what you want to get from the record of your collection, and you'll be amazed at how much more effective your results will be. And as your collection grows, you won't find that you've painted yourself into a corner, by not having given your record any room for expansion.

Photographs of your collection need to serve two purposes. The first is an effective pictorial record. These will be photos that can stand alone in an album, or be used to illustrate a website. These make an attractive bonus for you, and could be your 'shop window', if you wish, for other collectors or experts. The second is to provide an accompaniment to the written records that describe and define your collection – you've got the passion, so we're sure you have reams of written material on it! There is no reason why you shouldn't take good-quality photos that serve both purposes.

For keeping an effective record of your collection, you need an effective framework. A spreadsheet, such as Microsoft Excel, is ideal. In Project Three we described how you can combine words and numbers in Excel with photos. The process for creating an illustrated catalogue is similar, but this time you need to adopt a consistent method of arranging and entering all your precious, hard-won data.

Arrange columns in the spreadsheet to list data relevant to your collection. For example, you might use basic column headings such as Item Name, Item Number (if you number your collection), Description, and Date Acquired. Other columns can be used to describe details that are appropriate to each item in the collection (such as details of distinguishing marks, notes about damage, colour, or size).

For serious cataloguing tasks – and particularly where collections are extensive – there is a more powerful alternative to the spreadsheet: the database. Database software represents the next level up from the spreadsheet in the organizational process. Although not designed for many of the spreadsheets' calculation and numerical tasks, databases allow a much more flexible approach to data handling. You can produce custom layouts in much the same way as you might a handwritten record card, and as with those cards you can decide how much space is devoted to a particular part of the record (known as a field). So, for instance, you need only give a little space to enter a date but can define a large text panel for entering detailed descriptions. Databases really come into their own when you need to start searching. The rudimentary searching abilities of the spreadsheet are replaced with something altogether more powerful and comprehensive. Not only can we search for specific words, but we can also search for groups of records that meet certain criteria. If, for our teddy bear collection, we wanted to find all those bears that are golden brown, were made between 1901 and 1919 in Germany, and are no more than 25cm tall, we need only issue the appropriate request!

Be a FileMaker Pro!
Not only do database catalogues work more flexibly than spreadsheets, but their screen layout can be adapted to fit the data required. Designing a database using the current crop of dedicated applications, such as FileMaker Pro (*pictured*), is not as quick as customizing a spreadsheet, but it's just as simple once you get the hang of database terms and techniques. It's just a pity the database is often left out of all but the Professional edition of office software suites. If you can get your hands on a database, you'll find its power comes from the comprehensive searching tools. Most databases are general-purpose, but some are specifically aimed at cataloguing image files, and by adding custom fields they can also be used to organize your collection, with images to the fore as the ideal at-a-glance reference. You've the bonus with these of being able to keep track of your collections of photos as well as physical objects.

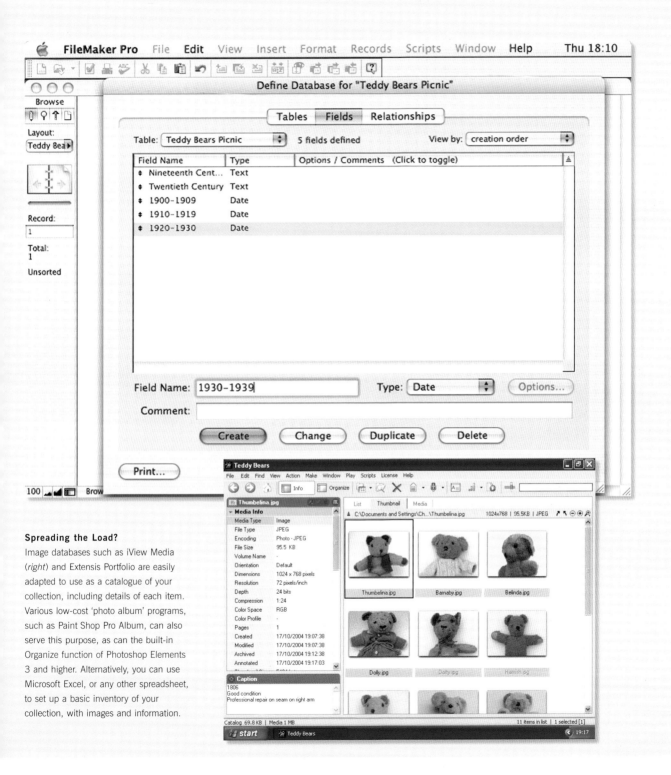

Spreading the Load?

Image databases such as iView Media (*right*) and Extensis Portfolio are easily adapted to use as a catalogue of your collection, including details of each item. Various low-cost 'photo album' programs, such as Paint Shop Pro Album, can also serve this purpose, as can the built-in Organize function of Photoshop Elements 3 and higher. Alternatively, you can use Microsoft Excel, or any other spreadsheet, to set up a basic inventory of your collection, with images and information.

Photographing objects in your collection is really a form of portrait photography. And if you've ever attempted to take proper portraits, you'll be aware what a problem it can be to light the subjects well. But photos of your *objets d'art* do require slightly different treatment. Rather than trying to produce a portrait that captures a person's 'essence', your aim here is to accurately record the subject neutrally. And the shadows that can give substance and form to portraits need to be banished, so that every possible detail of your subject is visible.

For a big collection, you'll save a lot of time by investing in a specialist lighting arrangement. Studio kits comprising two (or more) light sources along with stands, reflectors, and diffusers (which can be used in any number of possible configurations) are widely available, reasonably inexpensive, and work equally well for a table-top setup as for a studio. In our case we want to make particular use of the diffusers. These spread the light from our source (generally flashguns) over a wide area so that the subject is not at the mercy of hard shadows. Place one of these either side of the subject, and you'll have virtually 'flat' lighting, which is ideal for these purposes.

What about backgrounds? If you've invested in specialist equipment you may also have been provided with one – or more – background screens. With names like 'Colour Fantasy', 'Forest Leaves' or 'Desert Skies', you may be tempted to enliven your photos by using them. Please don't! Your bears will be forever lost in the woods. Although these are great for normal portraiture (and are the staple of many professional portrait studios), don't be tempted to apply such artistic flourishes. On a website in particular, they'll look cluttered and confusing. Stick to a plain, white background or, if you prefer, a soft, off-white. A plain background makes it much easier to view the subject, and will give you the flexibility to manipulate the shot digitally later.

The best way to achieve consistent lighting is to use a lighting 'cove'. A white-sided enclosure (normally made of translucent Perspex), this is designed to provide shadowless, even lighting. Commercial photographers who need to shoot products for advertising or promotion typically use these devices. And although commercial models command the prices that professional users expect, only simple carpentry skills are needed to build one yourself. By fitting a translucent top (or even leaving it open) and painting the whole interior white, you can achieve similar shadowless results for very little expenditure.

CHANGING THE BACKGROUND
You might not always want the same background for your photos. For example, you might want to colour-code them on a website (using different colours for different decades or manufacturers). Here we've used the Extract tool that we mentioned on page 51. It's only available in the full version of Photoshop, but is excellent for cutting out teddy bears because it's adept at handling furry edges. More basic selection tools will always retain some of the background between the hairs!

LEAVE ROOM FOR EXPANSION
Even if there are, ultimately, a finite number of objects to collect in your chosen field, it pays to keep your options open and allow for more entries in the future. Whether you use a spreadsheet or database application, you'll be able to make additional entries easily (as new rows or columns in the case of a spreadsheet, or new records in a database). With this in mind, it's important that your catalogue can accommodate future expansion – make sure that your planning has made allowance!

All Change!

Once you've extracted the image, you can paste it onto any other background. Note that there is no trace of the original light background – even in those 'difficult' areas in the fur. You can experiment with different colours to find one that best suits the subject, but in general it's a good idea to go for softer and more muted colours.

Spending a little time in preparation shouldn't just apply to planning the project as a whole. Time spent preparing to take the photos themselves can pay real dividends too. An extensive collection is going to take time to photograph, and at times you will feel you're on something of a production line. And with large numbers of photos coming from your conveyor belt, you'll want to keep any postproduction image manipulation to a minimum.

But inevitably there will be a few little jobs that need attending to after you've finished photographing everything. They might include small changes to contrast and brightness levels (our 'flat' lighting style is never 100% right for all subjects), and removing unwanted artefacts (like the fingers used for support in the illustrations opposite).

You could annotate your photos once you've pasted them into your spreadsheet or database, but you might also want to include captions on each image to give a unique reference or description. The filename of the photo is usually sufficient to describe the photo uniquely (matched with the corresponding record), but many people prefer the additional level of insurance that an on-screen identifier can provide. Adding text in your image editing application, perhaps in combination with lines and arrows to highlight one or more features of the object, is particularly useful if you intend to share the photos with others. Adding text is easy, but you should ensure that the text size is sufficient to be read, yet not so large that it intrudes on the image. It should also be of a neutral colour that makes it easily read. 'Sans serif' fonts (those like Arial and Verdana that have 'clean' edges) are easier to read on-screen and are preferable to 'serif' fonts (like Times and New Century Schoolbook), whose tails and flourishes often make them harder to read on a computer monitor.

SHADOWS ARE YOUR ENEMIES!

It's crucial to avoid deep shadows when taking photos of your collection, and the same applies if you're going to use these shots in a simple animation – even more on this shortly! But for a simple 'movie' of one of your collection, flat lighting is no longer sufficient; you'll need to move your diffused light sources further to the sides and introduce another to the front, in line with the camera. Viewed in isolation, the results you'll get from this form of lighting look a little absurd; it is shadows, after all, that help create the illusion of three-dimensionality in the subject. But don't worry: when compiled into a sequence, the shots will look fine! See page 106.

CHECK BEFORE TAKING THE PICTURES

How many times have you taken a photo, only to find when you examine the results that you've committed some howling gaffe? That tree apparently growing out of someone's head, or that missing limb, are just two examples of defects that could so easily have been recognized when composing or arranging the shot. When you're photographing your collection it pays to be equally vigilant. Don't just check in the viewfinder once; check again. And if you are using a digital camera, review your shots periodically so that you can correct any deficient images quickly. You will be able to fix many problems digitally later, but why bother when you can get things right in the first place?

REMOVING UNWANTED DETAILS

Sometimes you've no alternative. To display your objects to best effect you might need to use an improvised stand, or even, as here, a steadying hand. Removing the evidence is simple – if you've taken our advice and used a plain white background! Here we've used a Clone (or Stamp) tool in our image editor to copy colour from the background over the hand. Getting a good clean edge is easier if you use a selection tool to define the clone area.

There was no alternative to a steadying hand here, but...

...a little work with the *Clone* tool gives teddy all the support he needs!

PHOTOGRAPHIC HINTS AND TIPS

THE LONGER VIEW

What is the best lens – or the best focal length – to use when photographing your collection? Many cameras feature a modest, wide-angle lens as standard, which is ideal for capturing wide, sweeping landscapes or group photos in a confined space. Unfortunately, these are not ideal for photographing objects in your collection. Wide-angle lenses tend to exaggerate perspective. Faces, in particular, look unusually round when taken in close up, and although it might not be immediately obvious, the same problem will affect the photos in your collection. It's better to use a basic telephoto lens. If you are using a 35mm camera, look for focal lengths between 80mm and 125mm. On digital cameras (or compact cameras) with zoom lenses you'll need to set an intermediate focal length around two thirds of the way from the wide-angle setting (the precise focal length is not critical).

GET IN CLOSE

Most digital cameras feature a useful Macro setting that lets you get in really close to your subject. Switching to macro lets you fill the frame with a tiny detail, and if your collection already features small items (perhaps jewellery, or even stamps) you could find that the Macro setting is more or less essential for filling the frame with each object.

A SENSE OF SCALE

The downside of photographing each object in isolation is that you lose the sense of scale, and it's impossible to tell how large any item is. Consider placing something in the scene that restores the sense of scale. It could be a clearly visible ruler or, for smaller subjects, a coin. If you collect vintage cars, steam engines, or boats, you can assume their scale will be fairly obvious – unless you have a giant ruler handy!

The trouble with the photos we take for record purposes is that they are – to be frank – a little dull. Of course this, as we explained, is born of necessity. But collections are there to be enjoyed, so why not make the best of them? OK, so we've already shown how a photograph of our collected teddies has almost no photographic merit, but you can create some very effective alternatives.

One way is to create 'virtual shelves'. Once you've taken all your 'catalogue' photographs, you can line up all those standard, face-on views and blend them together seamlessly into a wide, panorama-style shot without any editing. And hope no-one sees the join! The consistent lighting and plain background should make this simple to construct. But an even easier way to compile selected images into a panorama is to use panoramic software – which would be particularly effective if you collect cars, for example, and line them up outside. But let's stick with our teddy bears. There are various economically priced packages for merging several images into a seamless panorama, such as Photovista Panorama (*www.iseemedia.com*) (available for Windows and Mac), and many image-editing programs, including Photoshop Elements, have the feature built in.

Panorama software can automatically identify common features in adjacent photos and blend them together. As our bear photos have no common elements (except for the white space), the feature will be unable to interpret these photos automatically, but it may work for your collection. In our case, we adjusted the subjects' relative positions manually. But with little effort, here's the result, *below*!

The Usual Suspects
Below Despite comprising eight individual photos, the resulting 'panorama' suggests that all eight were in the same line-up. So which one do you think hit Goldilocks?

STITCHING IN TIME

Panoramic software may be easy to use, but there are some complex calculations going on behind the scenes. For best results, you'll need to identify the focal length of the lens used to take the photos (perspective corrections differ with focal length) and provide a significant (around 30%) overlap between adjacent scenes. This gives the software something to lock onto when linking images. Joining the images – called stitching – is an automatic process, but most programs allow some manual intervention. This can be critical in cases where the software is unable to identify common points, or is confused by repeating patterns or similar features. If your panorama is wide enough, you can even produce a 360-degree view. When viewed on-screen you can circle continuously through your collection – and so can your website visitors if you post it online!

Whether strictly for recording purposes or more artistic interpretations, our object photographs only provide single viewpoints. You could include additional shots that show what lies around the back, but wouldn't it be great if you could display an object from any angle? Well, you can!

You can do this using virtual reality technology. This isn't the virtual reality that involves wearing special gloves and headsets, but thankfully (unless you like dressing up) a practical desktop variation.

This technology, made popular by Apple through its QuickTime VR software, allows the viewing of two types of virtual reality environments ('movies') – panoramas and objects. Both comprise still images. Panoramas are similar to the one we created on the previous page, except that when viewed through an appropriate player, the viewer can choose to move around the scene and even zoom in or out on certain elements. It puts you in the picture, at the centre of the action!

Object virtual reality movies place an object at the centre and, as if it were on a turntable, lets you rotate it to view from all angles. When you view a virtual reality object, the mouse pointer becomes a grab hand. Click with your mouse button and you can use this to drag the object around (nominally round a vertical axis, although triple axis all-direction rotations are possible too).

Creating an object movie involves photographing the object and then moving it around by a few degrees and taking another. You repeat until the full 360 degrees have been covered. The more photographs you take, the smoother the movements will be when the movie is played. At ten-degree increments the movie will be very jerky, while using two degrees will give a very smooth result (albeit with a large file size!).

Producing successful virtual reality is a complex process, but there are easier (and often equally effective) alternatives that you can attempt, such as the movie animation we describe, *right*.

DON'T FORGET THE CD!
Burning the photos and records of your collection to a CD serves two useful purposes. First, it ensures that you have a backup of all your important work, and lets you free up valuable hard disk space. Second, it provides a historical reference of your collection. As your collection grows, you'll be able to look back and check the changes, monitoring all those items you've added and, perhaps, recalling those long-departed ones that you sold or gave away!

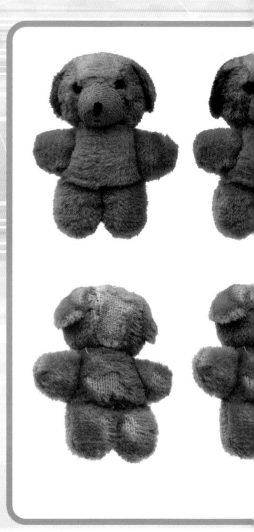

Round and Round
For a genuine VR movie, you'll need to photograph each object from every angle. Placing it on a turntable can help here (IKEA sells them cheaply!). Flat, shadowless lighting is essential to prevent strange artefacts, known as 'banding transients', spoiling the movie's quality.

MOVIES IN THE ROUND

Creating 'real' virtual reality movies is not that simple, and it can also be a laborious process. You can, however, achieve a very similar result by building an animation manually based on a sequence of photos. By using each consecutive photo as a frame of the animation and getting the resulting movie to loop continuously, you'll get an impressive effect. You could use an animation generator for this, such as Animation Shop, supplied with Paint Shop Pro, or Ulead GIF Animator, one of many packages that specializes in the GIF animation format. Alternatively, use a movie-editing application. Import each still image in turn, and set each to display for a short time (0.1 or 0.2 seconds).

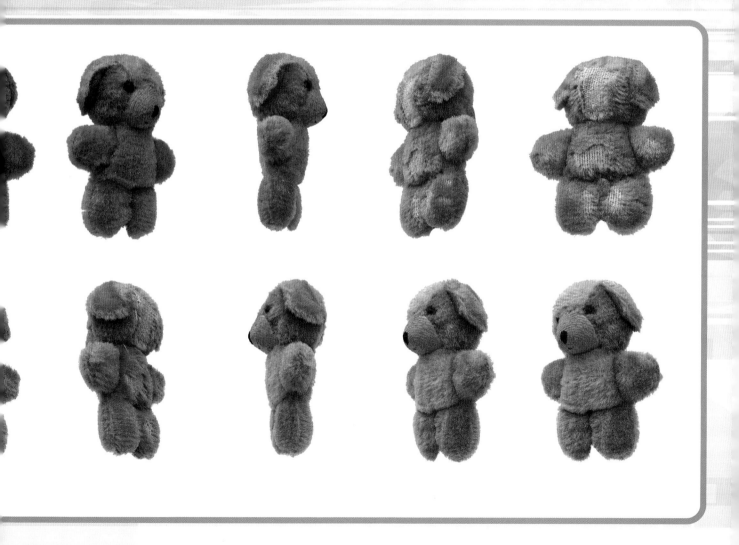

When you've finished recording your collection, you might be surprised at how valuable a resource you've created. Even if your collection is of obscure items of minor monetary value, you'll discover there are many other collectors out there. Be a collector of things of more bankable value, and you may find there are many more people interested in sharing your data.

The easiest way to share information is to create a web page. And as you've already created the photos to illustrate it and gathered the technical details, it will just be a matter of putting these together on the page.

It's important that the web page is constructed in a way that makes it easy (and obvious) for any visitor to navigate. Many a potentially useful site has been compromised by poor navigational tools, which make it impossible for visitors to get from one point to another intuitively. Website visitors have expectations based on other sites that they've visited, and they'll have scant patience for anything that isn't as slick!

Don't forget your website could contain not only the images you've created, but any research documentation you've found and links to other relevant websites. And if you've been bold enough to create a virtual reality movie or animation, why not include those too? Or links to your database? You could even consider including some video clips if the items in your collection are in any way 'animated'. Even items such as 'transforming' toys will benefit from the movie treatment, showing how they operate or change. It's easy: just set your video camera on a tripod and record the action!

DAY OF RECKONING

Your records could well have an unexpected use should something unfortunate happen to your collection. If you're unlucky enough to be robbed, suffer a fire, or some other material loss, then proving your loss to insurers and their adjusters could be a huge problem. How do you demonstrate the scope and nature of your collection, when there's no hard evidence of its existence? Your database and the photos in it could come to your assistance. Although they won't prove beyond doubt the details of your collection, they'll go a long way to help you make good. In fact, this is a good reason why you should make an inventory of your whole house. Obviously, it's not feasible to list every possession, but you can record much of the content in comparatively few photos.

1949-1959

Details ◯

1920-29   1930-39   1940-48   1960-66

Growing a family tree

Whether you're looking into your roots, seeking out an illustrious ancestor, or just plain curious, genealogy has never been more popular. And of all its aspects, the creation of a family tree has never been so easy. The Internet has given us the opportunity to email friends and family – or even see them, via webcam – as often as we wish. And this same technology has made it easy to trace family members, both past and present. So great is the range of information now available to us that you can go well beyond the traditional family tree and construct elaborate histories, complete with photos, videos, and documented details of work and home life. And with your newly honed digital scrapbook skills, you can bring your ancestors back to life! Although the web has provided a great many resources for the family history researcher, by no means all your material will arrive in this way. Most will come from current family members. Just think of the number of photo albums, many dating back decades, that are in the family. These are the ideal basis for your next project!

DON'T FORGET OLD HOME MOVIES!

Old collections of home movies are an ideal resource for discovering more about your – and your ancestors' – past. They will be full of family gatherings, social events, and travel footage that can give you valuable insights into your roots. And think of the resource you can leave your descendants! Why not hold a movie night and invite family members along? You can use the event to help identify your own movie's stars and give further substance to your family tree project. It's also a good idea to transfer old movies to digital video stored on CD, DVD or MiniDV tape. Give posterity a chance!

Check those Shoeboxes!

Those forgotten or archived boxes of old documents – collected in old shoeboxes, perhaps, or gathered from a house clearance – are a great source of information. Birth certificates and letters are an obvious source of important information, but other saved documents can give intriguing insights into the way your forebears lived. Something as humble as a bank statement could be a goldmine (literally, we hope!). You'll see how much your distant relatives were paid and how they used their money – even who they traded with. And wartime documents might give an insight into their lives through their darkest days. Receipts can provide useful provenance on family heirlooms – some of which may be in your possession today.

Picture Collections

Picture collections could be the backbone of your family tree project. Not only do they provide a glimpse of long-departed relatives, they're useful documents that show the way your predecessors lived – and dressed. Get the hair!

For many researching their family history, the excitement comes from the detective work. It will involve not only a search through family archives (which, in general, tend to extend to only a few generations), but local governmental agencies and church records (which tend to hold much of the historical data in many Christian traditions).

Gathering information from the Internet can be a problem – it isn't yet a cure-all for information ills. If you perform a simple surname search using one of the more comprehensive search engines (such as Google, AltaVista or Lycos), you're likely to get thousands of 'hits', even for less common surnames – most of which will be irrelevant.

So, as we covered in the introduction to this book, you'll need to be more focused. If you know your family has some roots in a particular location, search using both your surname and that location as keywords. You can also use one of the excellent genealogy 'portal' sites, which link to sometimes hundreds of other resources. These links and access points to further sites enable you to conduct a very precise and detailed investigation. Cyndi's List (*far right*) is a good example.

It also pays to be proactive. Set up your own website and invite others, perhaps distant relations who you may have discovered are investigating their own ancestry, to contribute. By including 'metatags' containing relevant words – perhaps surname, ancestors' names and home towns – in the HTML code of your website, you can help attract visitors who are using these same keywords in their own searches. (Find out more about metatags at *searchenginewatch.com*.) The aim is to inform others of your presence and get as much pertinent information as possible. Even a couple of paragraphs of text and some photos will get you started.

IF YOU DON'T ASK, YOU DON'T GET

Not all your information will be presented to you on the proverbial plate. You'll need to do some asking, and – in a few cases – begging! When the begging needs to be done of relatives, assure them that the valued documents or photos you're asking to borrow will be copied and the originals returned to them undamaged. Official records are often freely available – if you know where and who to ask. Depending on where you live, copies from the records kept by local, state, and federal government agencies can be obtained relatively easily. Those from churches and other nonstatutory organizations may involve a little cajoling. Perhaps a contribution to the upkeep of the church might help!

Colls of

Henry Colls of North Elmham
B   M. 1628 to Elizabeth
D. 1641

William Colls of North Elmham
B 1632   Husbandman
M. 1660 to Joanne [née Boyde
D 1673

William Colls of North Elm
B 1664   Water-mill owner a
          and later at Aldb
M - 1691 – Mary née Boyden
D - 1740 at Aldborough

Robert Colls of Itteringha
          Water-mill owner
B 1708 at Burgh   Left h
M - Hannah – B 1712 D1800
D - 1777

John Colls of Horstead marr
B. 1744   Water-mill owner
          at Horstead
M. 1767
D 1806   Grave stone on floo
          of Horstead church
          just inside door, on
          right

John Colls of Gt Yarmouth Ma
B 1771   Merchant
M. 1805 to Ann née Weeds
          Daughter of Capt. Jame

Windows on your World
Genealogical portal sites are a great way of beginning your investigations, and can alert you to new resources.

andman

ry Colls Prudence Elizabeth
  1630   Colls   Colls
 .1705
  William Banbury

Prudence Colls
h   B1669

nne Colls B1711 D1733 Eliz
eringham   B 1
rs mill at   D 1
rough in 1736

abeth   Anne Colls Hannah
Everard B1755   Colls
Sprowston   marriec
 –1811   William
                    Partrid
                    1762 Wi
                    remarr
                    1770 to
                    William

lls B1777 Hannah Colls Mar
ed William M. Thomas   N
  Mack   Thurtle of
 Farmer   Sculthorpe
t Annishland

FROM LITTLE ACORNS... FAMILY TREES WILL GROW

You may be fortunate enough to discover that your whole family tree has already been compiled by a zealous relative, but if not there is a good chance that some parts of it have indeed been documented. Such works could be residing in an official resource – such as local governmental offices or record offices – just waiting for you to uncover them. Others may have already found their way onto the web. Of course, how easy it is to find the information will depend on your surname – if yours is relatively common, you'll be facing much more of an uphill struggle to sift your relatives' details from those of thousands of unrelated strangers. It's very likely that your investigations will ultimately produce a mix of historic documents and web-delivered material.

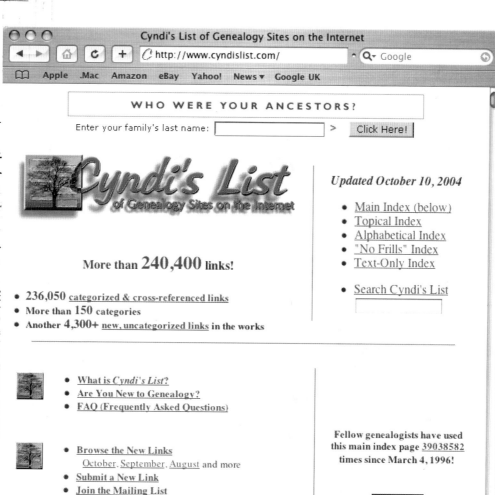

Cyndi's List of Genealogy Sites on the Internet

http://www.cyndislist.com/

Apple .Mac Amazon eBay Yahoo! News▾ Google UK

WHO WERE YOUR ANCESTORS?

Enter your family's last name: [   ] > [Click Here!]

Cyndi's List
of Genealogy Sites on the Internet

More than **240,400** links!

- 236,050 categorized & cross-referenced links
- More than 150 categories
- Another 4,300+ new, uncategorized links in the works

Updated October 10, 2004

- Main Index (below)
- Topical Index
- Alphabetical Index
- "No Frills" Index
- Text-Only Index

- Search Cyndi's List

- What is *Cyndi's List*?
- Are You New to Genealogy?
- FAQ (Frequently Asked Questions)

- Browse the New Links
  October, September, August and more
- Submit a New Link
- Join the Mailing List
  Browse or Search Archives

- Make *Cyndi's List* Your Homepage!
- Create a Link to *Cyndi's List*

Fellow genealogists have used this main index page 39038582 times since March 4, 1996!

Hosted by RootsWeb

As your investigations continue, you're likely to come up against some obstacles. Some of these will be difficult to overcome. There might, for example, be an abrupt break in the records, or the records might themselves be missing or have been destroyed. Others will be a simple challenge, such as the discovery that your ancestors or relatives had emigrated to or from other countries. Clearly, it's not feasible to visit each of these countries and continue your enquiries directly, so you'll have an ideal opportunity to test your web-investigative skills!

Some of the larger web portals can give useful pointers to websites to explore in other countries. A useful feature of many portal sites is their database collections. These list databases of official records – ranging from national census surveys through to local parish and probate records – that are available online and can be browsed by the researcher. Ancestry.com, for example, lists (or provides access to lists of) hundreds of millions of names from around the world, and has nearly a million subscribers. You can search through census records, military records, the Land Registry and Probate Office (for those with British ancestry), Civil War records, and more – much, much more.

Gathering information from so many sources is almost guaranteed to produce results. But if you are particularly successful, and discover a great number of relatives and ancestors, how far back should you go and how many strands of your family should you include? In many respects that's a very personal question. People have their own reasons for delving into their pasts, but as a rule of thumb most people tend to construct family trees that are deeper than they are broad. So you'll find more generations – the 'depth' of the tree – listed than parallel strands, which are those parts of the tree populated by 'removed' cousins and the like, who comprise the 'breadth'. People, it seems, are keener on seeing where and who they came from than discovering where distant cousins are now. Of course, there are exceptions. If you're convinced you are a distant relative of royalty, or share the genes of those in political power, broad trees will be essential.

Under One Roof

Websites like Ancestry.com act as both portal and search engine. Bookmark these sites and visit often, as new material and extended resources appear all the time – you may find that crucial database you have been awaiting has arrived. You can also opt to be emailed.

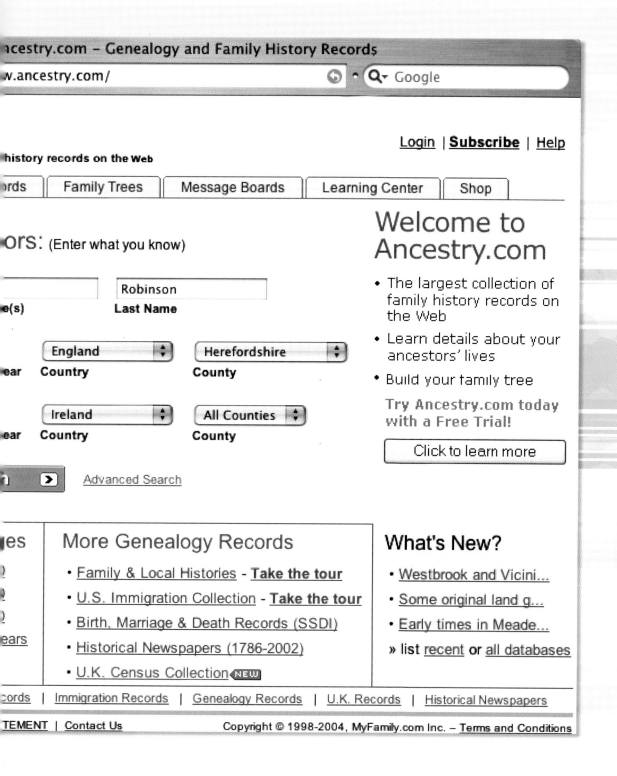

ncestry.com – Genealogy and Family History Records

w.ancestry.com/ | Q▾ Google

Login | **Subscribe** | Help

history records on the Web

rds | Family Trees | Message Boards | Learning Center | Shop

ors: (Enter what you know)

Robinson

e(s) **Last Name**

| England ▾ | | Herefordshire ▾ |
| ear **Country** | | **County** |

| Ireland ▾ | | All Counties ▾ |
| ear **Country** | | **County** |

❯ Advanced Search

Welcome to Ancestry.com

- The largest collection of family history records on the Web
- Learn details about your ancestors' lives
- Build your family tree

Try Ancestry.com today with a Free Trial!

Click to learn more

More Genealogy Records

- Family & Local Histories - **Take the tour**
- U.S. Immigration Collection - **Take the tour**
- Birth, Marriage & Death Records (SSDI)
- Historical Newspapers (1786-2002)
- U.K. Census Collection NEW

What's New?

- Westbrook and Vicini...
- Some original land g...
- Early times in Meade...
- » list recent or all databases

cords | Immigration Records | Genealogy Records | U.K. Records | Historical Newspapers

TEMENT | Contact Us   Copyright © 1998-2004, MyFamily.com Inc. – Terms and Conditions

Once you've collected your information and family history documents, it's finally time to start growing your tree. There are many software packages available to help you do this, but do you actually need anything other than a large sheet of paper – or word processor file? It depends on the detail you require. Pen and paper have served the genealogist for centuries, and examples of his or her art may well be in your family history portfolio. If your tree is to be equally simple, you could build it in anything from Photoshop Elements to Microsoft Excel, adding in old and new digitized images or subsidiary information, as you did in our pet calendar project (see page 48).

For a more ambitious project, dedicated family tree software has several advantages. Most significantly, it can make one of the more difficult tasks in any family tree construction – reconciling all the branches of the tree – simple. And you need only enter the names of the relatives to set up your basic framework. You can instantly print out the results. Or enter more information – facts, figures, or personal histories – relating to these. Pretty soon your tree will be blooming.

Virtually all genealogical software applications will also help you extend your search. By carefully analyzing the information you've already provided (such as the names, place and date of birth, and so on), these packages can search the appropriate databases and attempt to uncover further relatives for you to investigate. Bear in mind that British data such as census indexes is not available in such good quantities as its equivalent for the US, so you may face more leg-work.

Don't underestimate the power of assisted searches, though. For example, one of the most popular applications, Family Tree Maker, scours almost every genealogy-specific site currently on the Internet and finds those most likely to contain information pertinent to your searches. It can then help you study those sites for more clues to your ancestry.

Another plus point for family-tree software is its ability to track your data. As your tree expands, the number of resources that you've accessed in its construction can quickly grow, so managing them can become impossible. By keeping tabs on all the material you've searched, wasted effort is limited.

But for most of us the mechanics of creating the tree are only of peripheral interest – we want to see the end result! And you can produce stunning family trees with photos and illustrations. Some applications even produce chronologies and timelines that show the evolution of your ancestry and correlate family events with historic milestones.

Your New Family Friend

Family-tree websites and software packages can deliver more than an easy way of presenting your family history. They can enhance and increase your information trawling, and give you more ways to organize all that compiled data.

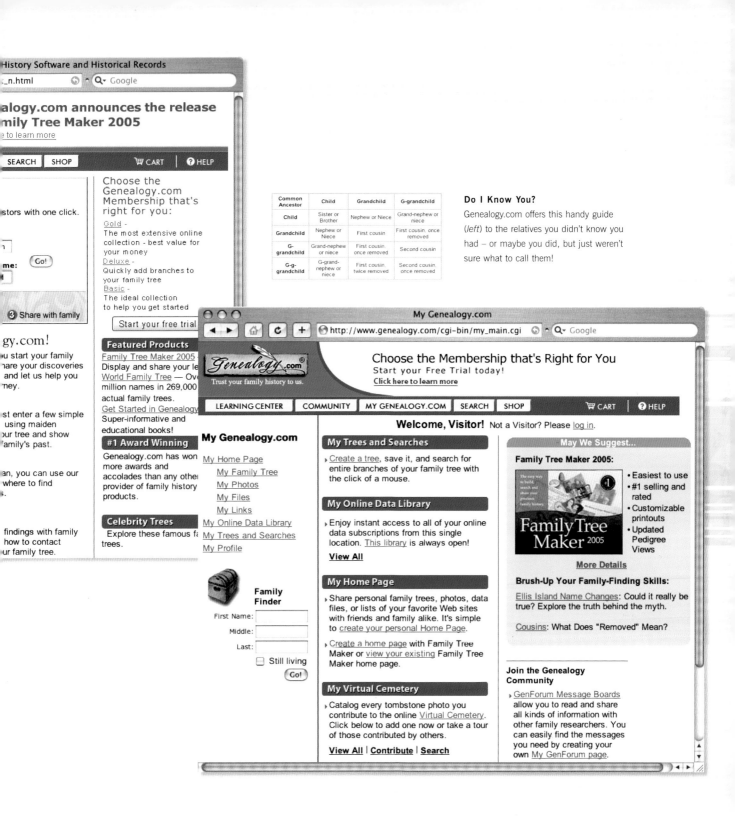

The success of genealogy sites has meant that there is now a high perceived value in the material contained in archives. So those who are used to the free (and some might say, anarchic) nature of the Internet might be in for some surprises. Access to many archive sites (whether through direct access or via a portal) is often on a pay-per-use basis. You might be charged for accessing the data and (in some cases) charged for printing out that data. If you request a hard copy to be sent to you from the originator, you will almost certainly be charged. If you think this unfair, consider for a moment the position of the originators of this data. They do not have to place this data on the Web; in doing so they are making the work of professional researchers easier. We, as the amateur sleuths of genealogy, have to work under the same rules. And you wouldn't begrudge paying to see the real records, would you?

If you find that you are making regular visits to information resources you might find it easier to subscribe to one of the portal organizations. These charge monthly or annual subscriptions and provide unlimited access to a set or collection of databases. There are no further fees to pay. Similarly, the vendors of many family-tree software applications provide the option of purchasing their products with the bonus of subscriptions to certain databases.

Family Tree Maker – the product we discussed on page 116 – includes a three-month subscription to Genealogy Library with one of its packages. This gives access to a range of researched family histories, marriage records, census indexes, and more. For a higher premium, you can include subscriptions to further databases, such as the 1900 Census and even International and Passenger Records – a vast collection of passenger lists, international censuses, and land records. But one note of caution. When you subscribe, do take care to check that those directories and databases to which you'll have access stand a good chance of being relevant. It may be of little value gaining access to the UK National Census of 1901 if your ancestry is entirely in Milwaukee, or the New York State Records if your family hails from London!

One particularly useful database to include in any subscription is World Family Tree. This is a vast searchable repository of family trees that researchers like you and me have contributed. You may be lucky and find several arms of your family already compiled in one of the trees here. Otherwise, paste yours and hope that it galvanizes others into action.

◄ ► 🏠 C + 🌐 http://www.cf-software.com/ ⟋ 🔍▾ Google

Cumberland Family Software
Family History Software for Beginners and Professionals!

Products | **Orders / Support** | **Miscellaneous**

▶ **Cumberland Family Tree** | ▶ **Other Products** | ▶ **Freeware**

FREE!

45-Day Trial Version of Cumberland Family Tree Pro

Current Version Pro 3.14

Discussion Group (Mailing List)
technical support and product discussion

To contact Cumberland Family Software:
ira.lund@cf-software.com

Professional Genealogy Research Assistance

Danish Research... Kay Lund Clark now does Danish Research. She reads and speaks Danish and lives in Rexburg, Idaho near a large LDS Family History Library on the Ricks College Campus. If interested please contact her at familysearch@ida.net

---

alogy Software: Index"

🔍▾ Google

to provide a link to Cumberland Family Software?
copy the gif banner below and include it on your
with a link to this page. Thanks for your support!

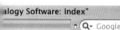
Cumberland Family Tree
Genealogy Software
For Beginners & Professionals

Editor's Choice Award PC Magazine

September 17. 2002
Legacy Family Tree 4.0
Deluxe Edition
Millennia Corporation

Deluxe Edition
Order your personal copy of Legacy Family Tree 5.0 Deluxe Edition for only $19.95 (download only) or $29.95 plus shipping and get the book and CD. more info

Buy Now

Upgrade to the Deluxe Version
Those who purchased Legacy 4.0 Deluxe Edition can upgrade to the New 5.0 Deluxe Edition for just $14.95

Buy Now

you track, organize, print,
erging, To Do list, slide

THE TRUTH IS OUT THERE

The Internet is a superb resource for gathering information, images, official documentation – you name it. 'Links' are what make the Internet function: billions of web pages are linked to billions of others, so your search could be literally endless. But it is also a useful way of 'following the scent' of an information lead, or tracking down loads of software packages that you might not find in the shops. But do a little research on what you're buying or downloading first. Is there a discussion board elsewhere on the Internet that rates the software? You'll almost certainly find that there is. And if the package you're considering using has hundreds of online critics complaining that it doesn't work, think twice before using it yourself. But most of the ones out there are fine – things don't last long online if they don't work. The Internet is good at 'regulating' itself in this way.

Once you've done your research and built the outline family tree, you can look at embellishing the material. Photographs begged, stolen (surely not!) or borrowed (of course!) from relatives will need to be copied. As you'll remember, a simple flatbed scanner will be sufficient for digitizing most conventional photographs. But also remember that many of these pictures – especially the older ones – will be quite fragile, so it's important to handle them with care. If the photos are mounted in an album and can't easily be removed, scan the whole album page and trim out any superfluous material later.

Time has two principal effects on your photos. It flattens the contrast through fading (which can occur even if the photos are stored in an album, away from the light), and also through the action of residual chemicals. Second, over long periods, it is almost inevitable that your photos will have suffered some physical damage. The corners get dog-eared, folds and creases develop, and, in the most severe case, the print gets torn. Fortunately, all these problems can be sorted digitally! You can boost the contrast (and, on old colour photos, even restore faded colour) and fix all those handling marks. You can finish with a photo that is better than the original!

THE FRUITS OF THEIR LABOURS

Photographs are an important element of any family tree. We compiled an illustrated family tree for this project – and we've been fortunate to discover photographs of the great-great-grandparents of the children shown in the tree (who, we suspect, might have grandchildren of their own by now, looking at their photographs!). We've even identified all the relatives in the intervening generations. When using specialist family-tree software, you'll often find that it's sufficient to save a photo to have it included in the tree. The software handles all the sizing, cropping and placement. And notice the structure of this family tree. We could call it a 'descendant' tree, as it illustrates all the descendants of the original couple, Joseph Reardon and Mary Hopkins. But you could base your tree on a selected child, for example, and trace their ancestry backwards.

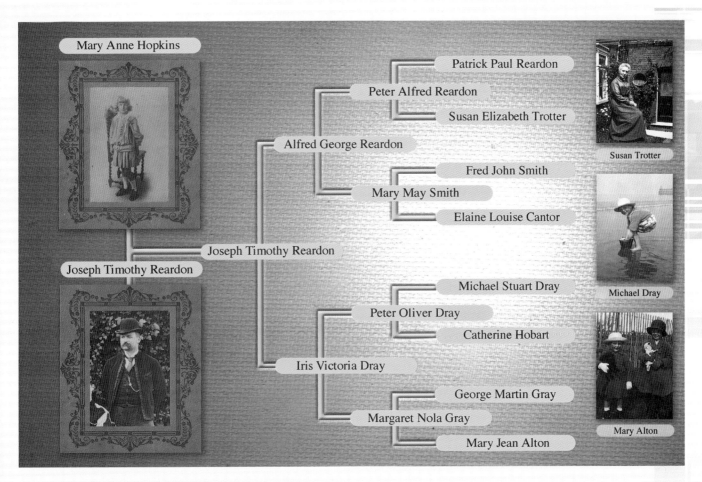

Mary Anne Hopkins

Joseph Timothy Reardon

Joseph Timothy Reardon

Alfred George Reardon

Peter Alfred Reardon

Patrick Paul Reardon

Susan Elizabeth Trotter

Mary May Smith

Fred John Smith

Elaine Louise Cantor

Iris Victoria Dray

Peter Oliver Dray

Michael Stuart Dray

Catherine Hobart

Margaret Nola Gray

George Martin Gray

Mary Jean Alton

Susan Trotter

Michael Dray

Mary Alton

Once you've created your tree, you won't want to keep your research to yourself – and no doubt those curious relatives from whom you've extracted information and ephemera will be keen to see the results. Printed family trees are fine, but a family website will be much more dynamic and can grow as more and more information comes your way. Like real trees, your family tree will never be 'finished'! And it will withstand the ravages of time, thanks to the digital skills you've acquired in this book. You've truly made something for future generations to enjoy.

A family website need not be just a collection of data, or a place that family members visit once to discover their own past; it can be an energetic forum through which far-flung relations can communicate, share stories, and develop a greater sense of belonging. Your website will rapidly become a family resource. It will be a place where news is shared; marriages and births announced; and biographies added. That's what digital scrapbooking is all about: sharing, preserving, editing, growing... giving a new lease of life to your precious memories.

JOB DONE!

This Constance-Barry family tree website is the result of a substantial amount of research. George and Susan Barry spent three years researching their ancestry, in the course of which they discovered a great deal about their ancestors and items important to their lives.

They've avoided the pitfall of merely pasting the family tree online, instead grouping the material into sensible sections. In this way, relations can find out more by exploring the site in different ways. For example, they could use the linear family tree as the start point, then branch off to discover more about particular relations. Or they could choose (by clicking on one of the 'saplings') to explore a selected time period, discovering more about the lives and times of their ancestors.

It's a site that's fun to visit and encourages people to visit again, and even add their own stories, anecdotes, and photos. Inspired?

Across the Pond

Families are fascinated by their roots, and when those are in another country, the story is more intriguing. Although the Constance-Barry ancestors were English, their descendants ended up in the US, where the family tree was compiled. Within the website, a short biography along with a few illustrative pictures brings each person to life. Visitors can click on each photo and see it enlarged, or even print off a high-quality copy for their own album.

the
Constance-Barry
family tree

Home ➡

• *Alfred George Barry 1892-1947*

Alfred Barry was born on the 6th of July and lived for the first part of his life in <u>Rochester,</u> Kent, England. He attended Sir Joseph Williamson's Mathematical School until the outbreak of the first World War, then became a junior medical officer in France until 1918.

After the war he married <u>Victoria Hoskins</u> and moved to <u>Maidstone,</u> Kent. Victoria gave birth to <u>May</u> in 1921 and <u>Elizabeth</u> in 1923. A son, <u>Charles,</u> was born in 1926 and emigrated to the USA in 1947. *More*

Pictures:

1800-1900

<u>Tea party</u>

<u>Victoria's home</u>

<u>St Luke's</u>

<u>Alfred's Aunts</u>

<u>Alfred Barry</u>

<u>Victoria Hoskins aged 9</u>

<u>Reginald Barry</u>

<u>Victoria aged 19 years</u>

Welcome to the
Constance-Barry
family tree

We've spent three years researching the Constance-Barry family tree and we think that the results so far have made it all worthwhile. We hope that you agree, and if you can help us further with our searches please don't hesitate to contact us.

  Some links are still nebulous but we are progressing steadily and will endeavour to update the site at least bi-monthly.

  We look forward to hearing from you,

George and Susan Barry

- Home page
- Site Plan
- Family Tree
- Album
- Surnames
- News
- Heirlooms
- Feedback
- Li...

Home ➡

1900-2000

---

the Constance-Barry *family tree*

Heirlooms

Just for fun we've included some pictures of the many artefacts handed down to us over the years. They're not particularly valuable as antiques but they mean a lot to us.

  *Every item has its own little story to tell and there's a brief description accompanying the photos. If **you** have anything of interest that you would like us to feature, please don't hesitate to get in touch.*   *More*

Richard Constance

1800-1900

May Barry

Peter Barry

Reginald Barry

Jack Constance

Keep it Light

There's a tendency for genealogy to become ponderous and academic. While some of the material may demand this, don't make it totally humourless. Here the Barrys have included a page of family heirlooms (one selected by each family member) that say more about the character of each person than they define the wealth of the family!

Decorative ideas: Rev those engines!

Over the next few pages, we're going to give your inspiration a kick-start with some decorative ideas for projects that could be part of a paper-based scrapbook, a website, or a CD. Then, in Section 3, we'll show you how to take your ideas a step further, and recap some useful hints and tips.

If a picture's worth a thousand words, imagine what you can say in a montage. A photo record of a sporting event could be interpreted in different ways. For example, we could get that fantastic shot of a winning touchdown or the victor's celebration. Trouble is, being at the right place at the right time to take the winning shot is something even sports photographers have trouble with. Another way is a photo collage that captures the flavour of the event. Getting photos for this is usually much simpler and more practical! Remember, in real life, there are no replays.

You should aim to get as many shots as you can of different elements. The event itself is of principal importance, but don't neglect other aspects. Photos of the crowd or spectators overcome with emotion, the pre-event build-up, and amusing incidents at the sidelines will all contribute raw materials for a terrific montage. Now try different ways of combining them. Import the photos into your image-editing application and create a collage. Depending on the pictures, you might want to tell a story, sequencing your images so that the day's events unfold. Or create a 'virtual stadium' with crowd scenes used to frame the montage of events from the field.

A Day at the Races

For this Porsche track event we wanted to convey the power and emotion of the day's racing. We took photos of the cars themselves and, by using relatively slow shutter speeds, created the impression of speed through panning and blurring. But we also photographed details of the cars to give a more comprehensive view of the day. Creating the montage also involved a little digital trickery. Some clip-art film stock has been used to simulate movie footage. Selected images have been pasted into the individual film frames. For the large central image, we applied Photoshop Elements' *Motion Blur* filter to the rear half of the car to suggest that the vehicle (which was parked!) was moving at high speed. Well, even the professionals sometimes cheat, you know.

Kids at play, the big catch

It's kids' party time, so informality is the keynote of this project. With colourful, happy shots of the little monsters, you can create an arrangement that really captures the atmosphere of the day. Spend some time getting the composition right... then spend just as long arranging and rearranging the images. That's the beauty of digital techniques: nothing's fixed until you say so. So don't worry too much about 'getting it right', but maybe start with the large images and then fill in the gaps with progressively

smaller ones. You can create the background either in an image-editing program such as Photoshop Elements, or in a vector drawing package like CorelDRAW. Alternatively, why not use one of the kids' own paintings as your background, and arrange the pictures on top? Above all, aim for a varied selection of images. Go for full-face portrait shots; group shots; grab as much colour as you can and really fill that page. And if you find you've any space, just drop another image in!

River Waveney 12/8/02 7.30am – 2.30pm Cloudy/bright Temp. 77f

Common Carp 12lb 2oz
Opposite club house,
30 yard cast, 12 ft
deep swim. Moderate to
fast flow.
Bait
Bread crust
Tackle
Float-leger, No 8 hook

Mirror Carp 10lb 6oz

Small island 100 yards
downstream of club
house, 4ft eddy,
left of dead tree.
Bait
Strawberry paste
Tackle
Swim-feeder, No 8 hook

Pike 14lb 3oz
(caught by Ralph!)

Road bridge, (right
of supports).
Bait
Yellow plug
Tackle
8ft rod, 12lb line

The Kids' Party

Without crafty image-editing tricks, we've achieved a result that looks a bit like a kids' pinboard that has been covered in photos. To further emphasize the fun nature of the project, we used a brush tool to give a big, splashy, party-style border to many of the prints. By applying *Bevel* Layer Effects in Photoshop Elements, these take on a more three-dimensional look. Splash! Now, where's Mum?

The One that Didn't Get Away

With an illustrated log book of a fishing weekend, there's less room for tall stories. A record like this says more than words could ever do. We've made a template then dropped the text and images onto it. The only image manipulation is a little cropping or resizing to ensure the photos fit the spaces. Then with bait and fish hooks ready, you've caught the day, as well as that fish!

You can just picture the day and imagine yourself dreaming by the riverside. This presentation's got it all: some lively pictures, found objects, a shot that establishes the sense of place – and all those statistics! Never again will he be able to say the fish was twice the size. Or will he? A few tweaks in your image-editing program, like Elements, and he could be holding Moby Dick instead of this less impressive beast. Go for a strong combination of graphics (from a drawing or image-editing application), text and photos. It's a good idea to be economical with text. Let the pictures tell the story – even if they're stretching the truth!

House, garden, and work

A great way of showing off a prized possession – whether it's an antique, a collectable, or a beautiful garden – is to combine the 'big picture' with smaller photos that pick out the details. But that's just the seeds of the idea. To really bring this garden into bloom, why not scan some of the plant name markers and use them as graphics to point out some of your pride and joy's best features? To make the smaller photos more prominent it's a good idea to use your picture-editing software to differentiate them from the background. You could, for example, put a drop shadow behind some of the smaller images, or tint the background (perhaps giving it an antique, sepia tone look). Here, though, we've chosen to give our main image a pale vignette to create some dynamics and movement, and to emphasize the light on this early summer's day. Turning the image into a web page could be the beginnings of

something much bigger: a colourful gardening website, with a page on each of the blooms, season by season. Photo stories are a staple of many magazines, and it's not too difficult to create one yourself. They're a great way of telling a story: a family day out, for example; or, as here, a typical day at work – just to remind you of what you've left behind as you put your feet up and get creative! You can always use some clip-art or stock photos to provide links in the storyline. Many graphics programs include (either in their drawing tools or clip-art collections) speech bubbles and text boxes that you can use to put words into your characters' mouths. If yours doesn't, you can create your own using the *Elliptical Marquee* tool in Elements, or whichever editing program you choose.

Over the Garden Wall

Creating a collage using layers in Photoshop Elements can really give your viewers a walk-through guide. Use this project as a start-off point for bigger ideas: a horticultural website; a month-by-month garden calendar as each bloom comes into season... even a small business website selling seeds, or gardening advice! Or just email your friends to show them how your garden grows...

The Working Day

You can easily make a photo story like this in your image-editing program (don't forget to save the whole thing as a JPEG for the web, or a TIFF for printing), or in a desktop publishing (page layout) program, or even, with a bit of patience, using a word processor. Clip-art images and graphics complete the story, or you can draw your own – or scan objects like tickets, bills, or paperclips.

Before and after, and the zoo trip

Why not combine your homemaking skills with your photographic expertise in this simple 'before and after' page? Combine it with the *Moving House* web project on page 56, and really tell the story of a house transformed, or 'burn' it onto CD to capture the whole experience for years to come. It's just what the professionals do: when interior designers and stylists set about transforming a room for their clients, they begin by assembling a 'mood board' featuring those colours, textures, and fabrics that

their clients have liked. Take a tip from this and include colour paint swatches and fabric samples (scanned on your flatbed) as part of the design. Of course, you don't need to restrict this idea to just a room makeover. You can use a similar composite to show the stages and end result of creating, say, a doll's house or any model-making activity. The techniques are the same: snap away with your digital camera as you go, grab those details, surprise your friends and family as they stumble around with boxes and cans.

Changing Rooms

Rather than a simple 'before and after' shot, this collage combines a large 'after' image with different views of the original room. Shots of the alterations in progress have also been included to illustrate how the transformation came about. Notice how swatches of the paint and fabric selected for the new room scheme were also scanned and have been included to complete the picture.

Origin of the Species

Photo collages of wildlife collections can often degenerate into a 'survival of the fittest'-style mess on the page. By keeping photos of similar fauna together and using a background appropriate for each group of subjects, images that might otherwise be confusing become much more powerful. The use of close-ups and different shaped images adds to the composition.

Then assemble it all later at your leisure – while someone else does the hard work!

Collections – of any sort – make ideal subjects for digital photo collages (as we saw in Project Eight), but to show them to best effect requires a little more imagination. Digital imaging techniques give us a host of inspirational tools that we can employ, from the simple (such as cropping selected photos into circles) through to complex blends in which disparate subjects are combined into a single scene. Another way to group like subjects into 'families' is to digitally paste them onto an appropriate background. This could be a colour or a texture that makes the subject look completely in its natural habitat. Are you in yours yet?

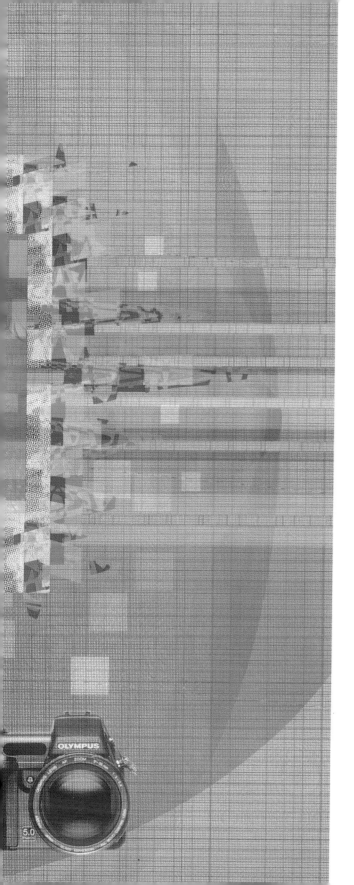

Hints and Tips

As you've worked your way through this book you'll have seen how powerful digital image editing is, and what a useful tool it is for making timeless and beautiful scrapbooks – then taking them to the next stage by publishing them online, or putting them on CD. But before embarking on any project it's a good idea to take a step back and assess the requirements of your raw material: your photos, videos, and memorabilia. Consider for a moment what needs to be done before they can grace your project. Throughout this section we'll examine issues such as these – and many more – and even look at some further uses for your masterpieces!

Taking better pictures of people

People are undoubtedly the main subjects of photography. Whether you're professional or amateur, people usually make the most compelling subjects. For most of us that compulsion is driven by emotions. We want, for example, to photograph important events, such as birthday parties and weddings that are meaningful to us. But of course it's the memories – rather than the photographs themselves – that are most important to us, so we're often indifferent to the quality of the shots we take. This is a shame, as the best photos – or the best use of those photos after the event – will take on the greatest significance as time goes by.

One of the biggest problems with photos of people is not getting in close enough. Although it might not be possible to get physically close to your subject (if they are taking part in a play or a sporting event, for example), you can make them appear larger. Use your camera's zoom lens (or switch to a telephoto lens if you are using an SLR) to ensure the subject is large in the viewfinder. If this really isn't possible, you can just select a detail of the image in your editing software and compose the picture 'after the event'. Shooting from a distance also makes the subjects less self-conscious, so you've a better chance of capturing their natural expressions.

It's always a good idea to shoot people using either a modest telephoto lens or a zoom lens set to an equivalent amount of magnification. Photographing people in their natural setting – whether at work or home – can also make for better portraiture, whether you're aiming for formality or informality. People are always easiest to photograph when they're at their ease, or on home territory. Taking pictures of people at work also lets you include some of the tools of their trade that add character to the shot.

Lighting

The way our subjects are lit has an important bearing on the quality of the photos. Shoot with the sun behind the subject, and you tend to get a dark silhouette that professionals call 'contre-jour'. Portraits like this are usually unflattering, and the background is often washed out as the camera's metering system tries to adjust to the brightness of the subject. You could use flash to equalize the lighting, but still the results are rarely satisfactory. Positioning the sun behind the photographer will give you much more even lighting, but it carries the risk that, if the lighting is strong, it can cause facial shadows and make your subject squint. The best lighting is when the source is positioned off to the sides of the photographer, though still forward of the subject. This gives sufficient shading to prevent dazzling the subject, but also produces flattering shadows.

Groups

Formal group photos have their place. Even the most avant-garde of wedding photographers feels obliged to include some 'stereotypical' shots in his or her clients' portfolios. The problem with group shots is often not the formality of the composition, but the lack of intimacy. Getting a good group shot requires the photographer and the subjects to be comfortable and relaxed with each other. Only then can warmth radiate from the photo!

Improving photographic technique

Digital image-editing can – in extreme cases – turn the proverbial sow's ear into a silk purse, but it still makes good sense to get your photos right in the first place. This means ensuring that when your eye is at the camera viewfinder, you take note of and appreciate your subject. Don't click the shutter straight away (unless by hesitating you're going to miss something crucial!); check around the frame to make sure you have the best composition. Check the focus. Is the subject in focus, and if so, how much of the foreground and background do you want to be in focus too? What about the shutter speed and exposure? Are these ideally set for your subject? Here are a few tips to point you in the direction of great photos.

The Rule of Thirds

We have an instinctive desire, when photographing any subject, to place that subject at the center of the frame. We have a similar desire in landscape photography to position the horizon dead center in the frame. But neither of these is, in compositional terms, ideal. Although you shouldn't let your photography be compromised by rules, there is one very good one that can help your compositions enormously: the 'rule of thirds'. Divide your frame into three equal segments horizontally and vertically. When taking landscapes you'll get much better compositions when your horizon is one third down from the top (or two thirds down, if you're recording a skyscape). Similarly, a portrait is best when the eyeline is one third down. The strongest compositions of all are produced when the principal subjects are placed at the intersection of these imaginary third-lines.

Depth of Field

Any lens is capable of producing a sharp image at just one distance. Only at this distance will the subject be absolutely sharp. But by reducing or 'stopping down' the lens aperture we can increase this range so that parts of the scene in front of and behind this point are also in focus. Cheaper

cameras have smaller apertures, so in the average family snap both the foreground and the background are in focus. One drawback of using small apertures is that a correspondingly smaller amount of light is admitted, so a much brighter scene is required unless your camera can use long shutter times – and you can keep it still during them! (Remember, special effects aside, more light generally means a better picture.) 'Depth of field' effects, where only objects at a specific distance are in focus, can be used creatively to isolate a subject from its surroundings. By using a larger aperture, we can blur the foreground and background and concentrate attention on that subject. Note that it's also possible to create or enhance depth-of-field effects in your image-editing software – an example is shown on page 141.

Shutter Speed

When a camera is used in *Auto* mode, we often pay scant regard to the shutter speed setting. But for some subjects – such as fast-moving vehicles and sports – it's important to get the shutter speed right. To 'freeze' the action, you need to ensure the shutter speed is as high as possible. If you're using a film camera, high-speed film, such as ISO 400, is helpful as well (specialist shops will sell you films as fast as 3200). To blur the action to give the impression of motion, you can use a slower shutter speed, as the portrait *above* shows. To get a sharp image with a longer shutter time, it's important to use a tripod or some other kind of camera support so that the image isn't spoilt by camera shake while the shutter remains open.

Exposure Control

Automatic controls also tend to adjust exposure settings so that an 'average' level is achieved. That's fine for most subjects, but some require different treatment. For example, photos of skiers and snow scenes taken using normal exposure settings will be dull-looking. Conversely, shots of richly coloured sunsets can often become washed-out as the camera compensates for the low light conditions. If your camera allows, you can change the settings manually or dial in an override amount, usually calibrated in 'stops'. For bright scenes, decrease the exposure by one or two stops. For dimly lit scenes, increase the exposure by a similar amount. Bear in mind that digital cameras don't cope well with very low lighting, generating a lot of 'noise' that lacks the romantic quality of true film grain. This portrait was taken with a slow exposure, with low ambient lighting and a directional spotlight.

Guide to scanning

Digital cameras have made it possible to take a photo, download it to a computer, and begin editing it within minutes. But what about all those other pictures you've taken over the years with conventional film-based cameras? And what about all that memorabilia? To edit materials like these, you first need to convert each item into a digital image – one that can be loaded onto your computer.

For this we need a flatbed scanner. These scan photos (or any other flat artwork, documents, and even fairly flat objects) line by line, building up a digital copy of the original in exactly the same way as a photocopier. You can set the scanner resolution, within the capability of your particular scanner, to determine the amount of detail recorded. To show an item at actual size on a webpage you need to scan at around 90 dots per inch (dpi). For printed output you'll need a higher resolution of 300dpi, for the reasons we explained on page 21, or 600dpi for black-and-white documents that you want reproduced really sharply. Most scanners can scan at a much higher resolution than this to capture maximum detail and allow you to scale images up. If you scan larger than you need, you can resize the image smaller for web use in your image-editing software.

Extra resolution is especially useful when scanning negatives and slides, which are usually smaller than printed pictures and therefore need to be scaled up more. To scan these transparent media you need a backlight, often provided within the lid of a flatbed scanner, known as a 'transparency hood'. You'll usually remove a cover to reveal it when required. Naturally, your negatives will also be transformed into positives!

Performing a scan is simplicity itself. Place the original, face down, on the glass plate. Press the Preview button (either in the scanner software or on the scanner itself) to make a quick rough scan, then select the exact area you want to capture. The final scan will take between a few seconds and a few minutes, depending on the resolution and area.

Slide Rules

Many flatbed scanners (*above*) can also handle transparencies, but only a dedicated slide scanner will give top-quality results from small-format originals such as slides. Most models accommodate 35mm, and, via an adaptor, APS (Advanced Photographic System) film. This Minolta DiMAGE (*right*) offers 5400dpi resolution, enough to get a 40-megapixel image from a slide! Professional models can also take medium- and large-format transparencies. Many slide scanners can auto-load batches of slides to save you time.

THE PICTURE CD

Scanners are versatile devices that have applications beyond photography, but if you don't have one and can't justify the purchase, can you still edit your film-based photos? Yes! Most photo labs (including those that operate by mail order) will copy slides, negatives and perhaps even existing prints onto a CD, either in Kodak's PictureCD format (left) or as a normal CD-R containing high-resolution JPEG or TIF images. You can then open and edit your photos directly from the disc.

Improving images

Some image problems and defects seem to occur with alarming regularity. Whether or not it's through poor camera technique, we often end up with photos that are slightly unsharp, or perhaps have a poor colour balance or even an unsatisfactory depth of field. But the good news is that image editing techniques let us improve these – and others – usually with a few mouse clicks, and a little application of intelligence, taste, and good judgment. Don't forget that when you're working digitally you can try any effect you wish, and, if you don't like the result, return to the original and begin again. So you can embark on flights of fancy in the certain knowledge that you're not compromising your valued photo collection!

SHARPENING

Let's be clear from the start. If your photo is blurred, whether through poor focusing or camera shake, you can't restore focus digitally. However, you can improve the perceived sharpness of an image. So what's the difference? When an image is in focus, lots of fine detail is visible. When an image is slightly out of focus, this detail is lost. Even an excellent photo may be slightly 'soft', especially if it's been scanned from a slide or print. Sharpen filters make soft edges appear sharper by increasing the contrast on either side. They can't do much for photos that are blurred, but can give extra clarity and immediacy to those that are well focused. Your image-editing program will offer several sharpening tools, but the most useful one is Unsharp Mask, or USM. The mechanics of this filter are rather complex, but the basic principle is that you increase the Radius setting until you get a visible improvement without creating artificial 'haloes'. Start with the Amount at 100% and adjust if necessary; the Threshold setting should be zero, but can be increased if grain is over-emphasized. The standard Sharpen filter is only useful at low resolutions.

BLURRING

If you've been working hard at getting your images sharp, you're probably wondering why you'd want to blur them. In fact, you rarely need to blur an entire image, but you can get fantastic results by creatively blurring selected parts. For example, you can select and blur parts of the foreground and background to emphasize depth of field. If you want to reduce the depth of field in a photo, you can progressively blur those parts of the scene 'away' from the subject. Other blur filters allow you to simulate effects such as using a motorized zoom lens to zoom out during a shot, or even blurring the wheels of a car to make a stationary vehicle appear to be moving!

COLOUR QUALITY

If you were able to compare your favourite photo with the original scene, you'd probably be surprised by how different the colours in your 'perfect' print were in comparison. There are no absolutes when it comes to photographing the colour in a scene, and our eyes and brains are pretty tolerant in accepting colours that are approximately correct. But there are limits, and we often cross these when photographing subjects that are unusually lit. Indoor scenes lit only by normal tungsten lights often take on a salmon pink tone, while fluorescent lighting can cause all manner of colour casts. Sometimes we want this cast, because it might convey a certain feeling (such as 'warmth' in a candle-lit scene), but more often than not we want a more neutral result. Digital image-editing software provides easy fixes to colour casts. Photoshop Elements' Color Cast command lets the user identify part of a scene that should be white or neutral and then adjusts the colours accordingly. This is particularly useful in removing non-standard colour casts. The alternative Color Balance command enables the balance between colours to be manually altered. For example, reducing the amount of red and yellow in a photo will reduce the colour cast due to tungsten lighting.

Retouching old photographs

Retouching old photographs has been one of the fields most significantly advanced by digital imaging, and for a long time the techniques were jealously guarded. Now that the mystique has been blown away, just about anyone can give old photos a second lease of life. And with the tools currently available you can achieve results that are even better than the original would have been when it was first printed.

When you digitally retouch a photo, of course, you're not doing anything to the original photo. Rather, you first scan the photo (typically using a flatbed scanner) so that you have a digital copy on your computer. The original photo can be returned to its album or frame and be enjoyed in its own right even after an enhanced version has been produced.

AUTO EVERYTHING

Where a photo has no physical damage but is faded or discoloured, you can use automatic correction tools to effect a quick restoration. These tools (which masquerade under names like Auto Enhance, Auto Fix, or Auto Correct) work by analyzing the photo to determine the range of colours, tones, and brightness, then adjusting these to give an 'ideal' mix. Although few photos conform to an ideal pattern, the results from using these tools are, in general, remarkably good, and some give you a range of options to choose from. The tools won't rescue the hopeless cases, but to make quick adjustments they take some beating, and might at least make an image usable, if not picture perfect!

Before…

…and after!

Old Retainers... Renewed!
Old photos fade, or become torn or
damaged. Even colour pictures from the
1970s will be showing their age by now.
But with the aid of some of the retouching
techniques explored below, you can not
only turn back the clock and undo the
damage, you could end up with a better
picture than when it was originally taken!

The first step in retouching a photo is one of assessment.
You need to look closely at the picture and establish exactly
what needs to be done. Depending on the state of your
original, you may need to:

• Replace missing parts. An old photograph that has been
  badly creased may have broken into pieces, some of which
  may not have been kept.

• Repair tears and creases. Even if the photo is still in one
  piece, there may be surface damage that needs attention.

• Remove dust and scratches. More superficial marking
  can be due to dust and scratch marks that might date
  back to the original printing of the photograph, or have
  accumulated over the years. And there may even be some
  new ones due to dirt on the scanner!

• Adjust the contrast, brightness, and, if appropriate, the
  colour. With all other damage corrected, you can boost flat
  contrast, alter the brightness, and even correct faded or
  distorted colour.

The first three steps involve the *Clone* or *Stamp* tool,
and/or, in the case of recent versions of Photoshop and
Photoshop Elements, the *Healing Brush*. In the case of missing
parts, you can sample pixels from other parts of the background
to make good the missing sections, in much the same way that
we used the foliage background to obscure a wedding guest in
the example on page 81. Where the missing section includes
part of the main subject (rather than the background), you'll
need to be a little more cunning and use a fine *Clone* or *Healing
Brush* to 'paint' detail back in using appropriate pixels.

You can attend to tears and scratch marks by cloning
pixels from either side of the damage. It's a good idea to blend
the colours either side of the tear. Set the tool's opacity to
50% to overpaint the original cloning work using pixels from
either side to achieve this, or consider feathering, smudging,
or slightly blurring the edges (see your software's instruction
manual). Smaller blemishes can be attended to simply by
dabbing the *Clone* brush over the marks using nearby pixels.

Finally, use the *Levels* or *Curves* adjustments (*Brightness*
and *Contrast* are usually less successful) to restore the look of
a pristine print. The last step will often be an *Unsharp Mask*
to make the picture look clearer than the original ever did.

Capturing video

The main reason digital video is promoted so intensively is its quality. Promising near-broadcast quality with a high-quality video capture card (a euphemism for 'very good indeed'), it is equally suited for recording family occasions as it is for semi-professional work. Other pluses include the compact size of the camera (many models are pocket-sized, if your pockets are deep enough to buy them), and the ease with which video recordings can be edited using a computer.

This is all well and good, but what if you have an analogue video camera? Or what if you own a digital video camera now, but have a large collection of video recordings made on earlier, non-digital tape? No problem: you can use these tapes almost as easily.

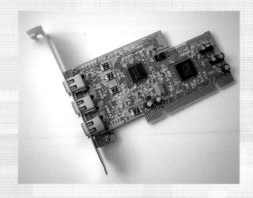

Plug and Play

Almost all recent Apple computers have FireWire sockets, but many PCs don't. If that includes yours, don't worry: third-party cards providing several FireWire ports are cheap to buy and easy to install. If you're not comfortable fitting it yourself, a local computer store should be able to oblige. Some video-editing programs are also available as a 'bundle' with a FireWire card.

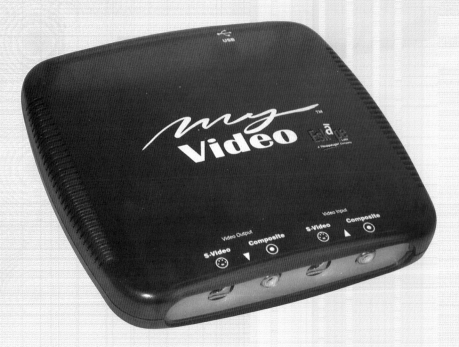

USB Capture Devices

Although USB connections (even the faster version 2) aren't fast enough to handle digital video, they can cope with analogue video transfer. Converters such as this are designed both to transfer video recordings and to play conventional television programmes on your monitor (given a suitable aerial connection). Like other A to D converters, these are bidirectional devices that also let you output edited video material back to analogue.

From A to D

Compact and easy to use, A to D converters make it simple to convert your historic collection of video recordings to digital, ready for editing. Once you've edited your video footage, you can also copy your edited version back to your VCR to store it on analogue VHS videotape.

To edit analogue video requires an extra piece of equipment known as an analogue to digital converter – or A to D converter for short – which converts an analogue signal into a digital one; in other words, one that your computer can understand and interpret in the same way as an original digital recording. A to D converters come in two flavours. One, perhaps the neatest, is a circuit board that you install inside your computer, in one of the its expansion slots. This provides connections for your analogue video camera (or VCR) and feeds the digital signal directly into the computer.

If you don't have any expansion slots free – perhaps you use a low-end laptop or notebook computer, or already have a lot of accessories – or you don't fancy opening your computer to insert the card, you can also buy external A to D converters, like those seen *above* and *opposite*, that connect to your computer via a USB or FireWire cable. These small desktop peripheral devices are often smaller than an external disk drive. You connect your analogue camera or VCR to the box, and you're ready to go.

No special video or electronic skills are needed to use these devices. The operating details vary according to model and type, but many models act like – and are seen by video-editing software as – digital video cameras. So you can import video footage in much the same way, and with applications such as Apple's iMovie (on the Mac) you'll even find that imported scenes are divided into video clips in exactly the same way as with a digital video recording.

It's as easy as A to D!

Combining video
and sound

Whether you've used digital video, or, as we described on the previous page, converted your analogue footage to digital, once you've imported your recordings and started editing you're going to want to produce a top-notch movie. In our wedding video project we examined the ways in which we could embellish the basic edited recording by using special effects and transitions. To make our production complete, we need to look more closely at the opportunities offered by video -editing applications with regard to sound.

Our edited video will already contain the live soundtrack that was recorded along with the original footage. 'CD quality' is the claim you'll hear over and over again for digital video sound. True, digital video as a technology is capable of recording sound to the standards of CD music recordings. However, while the sound circuitry is capable, the devices – principally the microphones – that we use to provide the audio signal are rarely up to anything like the same standard. Built-in microphones are competent all-rounders, but, like most all-rounders, do not excel in any area.

So we suggest investing in an auxiliary microphone. The most useful of these are optimized both for recording sound directly ahead of the camera (where your action takes place!), but also for recording some of the sounds around it (so-called 'ambient' sounds).

Once you've compiled your video, even if you've used a top-grade microphone for great audio quality, you'll find that scene transitions can be problematic as far as sound is concerned. When you insert a fade or crossfade, you'll find the sound fades as well to match the visuals, while the sound during ordinary, abrupt scene transitions changes equally abruptly. Obviously this is far from ideal, and will lend your video an unnecessarily amateurish feel. Video-editing applications should provide the means to fade the sound in a clip, but often this is an equally unsatisfactory solution. A more effective way is to use a

Sound Performance?
Given their size and positioning, the microphones built in to virtually every video camera do a remarkable job. But they're something of a compromise, and as such are not ideal for all occasions. There's also a strong risk that, being integral to the camera, they may pick up the sound of the tape mechanism's motor, and even that of the zoom lens if you use it during the recording.

The Auxiliary Mic
Although an auxiliary microphone adds bulk to your digital video camera and affects its handling, the pain is certainly worthwhile when you hear the results. Models such as this are available with standard response (that is, they are optimized to pick up those sounds immediately in front of the camera) and 'zoom' response. Somewhat inaccurately named, zoom models are designed with particular sensitivity for a small area in front of the camera in order to pick up more distant sound – handy for when you can't get next to the action.

good piece of background music that, having being recorded independently of the video material, will be continuous and lessen the impact of any gaffes in the original soundtrack. You'll find many sources of background music on the web, including useful 'looping' music that plays continuously with no obvious break. Importing these – or any sound files – into your video-editing application is simple, and the imported track can be moved around timeline just like the video clips. You can even apply fades at the start and finish.

Sound Mixing

With two audio tracks (in addition to the soundtrack with the video footage), each of which can fade independently, it's easy to add background music and sound effects in Apple's iMovie. You can use the same tools as are used for editing the video to achieve frame-accurate precision in the placement of the sound files.

Animation and graphics

If you want to add a little extra spice to your digital scrapbook projects, whether you're publishing them on the web or burning them onto CD, then why not add some basic animation? It's not as daunting as it sounds. If you can generate a simple graphic, then in many software packages you can animate it too. You could even scan a kid's painting, a party hat, or a photo of a friend, and make it the raw material for a quick animation. Imagine the kids' party project on page 126 with a clown's face bouncing across it, or a succession of images in the fishing project on page 127, showing the catch being lifted out of the water!

Animations are perhaps the most obvious attention-grabbing features on websites, and are easily constructed in applications like Paint Shop Pro and Ulead GIF Animator as well as more professional web tools such as Adobe ImageReady and Macromedia Fireworks. There's also dedicated (and complex) software for producing 'vector-based' animation in the Macromedia Flash format which many users' browsers can play.

As you've surfed through websites, you'll have seen that animations can vary from the simple and basic through to complete virtual environments. The most common format is GIF animation. GIF (Graphics Interchange Format), a standard image file format, also permits animation, and its small file sizes make it ideal for delivery via the web.

A FLASHY ALTERNATIVE

GIF animations are often seen as being rather basic and lacklustre. That's mostly just because too many people have used the format for lazy work, but it's true that long or complex animations don't suit it well. For the best in animation you'll need to use Flash, the name both for Macromedia's vector animation technology and its software for creating animations in this format. It's not a cheap option, and it takes time to learn both the software and animation skills, but the results will amply repay your efforts.

ROLLOVERS

You've probably made good use of website rollovers without realizing exactly what they are. You'll have noticed buttons, menus or other 'hotspots' on a website, where moving the mouse cursor over a particular item makes the underlying text or graphic change in some way, and it then changes again when you click – for example, from plain to coloured, or to a 'pressed button' embossed effect. That's a rollover. They're used to acknowledge that you're on an 'active' area of the website, and that clicking will activate a link. The imaginative website creator won't be happy with a simple change of colour; they'll want something more dramatic and creative. You can create exciting rollovers in much the same way as a GIF animation. Using the *Rollover* palette in your web design or image-preparation software, you can determine the look of the rollover for *Normal, Mouseover, Mouseclicked*, and other 'states'.

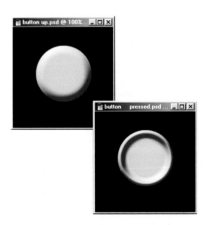

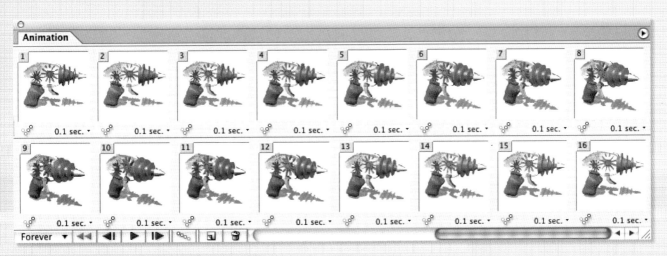

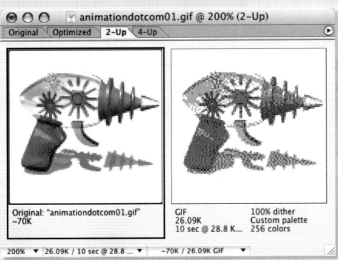

Original: "animationdotcom01.gif" ~70K

GIF
26.09K
10 sec @ 28.8 K...

100% dither
Custom palette
256 colors

Small Wonder

Just like still images, animated GIFs can be compressed to varying extents to balance quality against file size. This example (from the large collection available by subscription at www.animation .com) has been optimized to 70K – not bad for 16 frames – but could be squashed even further.

GIF ANIMATIONS

GIF animations are widely seen on the web, partly because they're easy to deliver and partly on account of the many tools available to create them. The full version of Adobe Photoshop includes an animation generator in its companion product ImageReady (*top*), and many Windows image editors such as Paint Shop Pro can also produce GIF animations, while other programs specialize in this task. The end result is simply a sequence of images, stored in the same file, which display in turn when it's loaded (for example into a web browser). So the process of

making a GIF animation is a bit like conventional cartoon animation, laying down 'cels' that correspond to each still frame of the animation. When these are displayed in rapid succession, they create the illusion of motion. Alternatively, you can set them to display for longer, like a slideshow. Most animation tools can also 'tween' – that is, generate images 'in between' two frames – so, for example, you could draw a ball in two different positions and move smoothly between them. You can specify the 'delay' time for each frame independently, and set the animation to play a certain number of times or repeat forever.

Outputting to non-traditional media

Digital images have a wide range of applications, as you've seen throughout this book. You can write them to CD, or even DVD; post them on a website; email them to your friends and family, or compile a truly innovative scrapbook from your efforts, with just a little imagination and confidence.

But as you know, digital means infinitely editable, and once something has been digitized and turned into all those exciting ones and zeros that can be sent from one side of the globe to the other in a matter of seconds, you'll discover that it can be output onto a thousand and one different things. For example, special transfer papers enable an image to be printed onto fabric, such as a T-shirt, simply by ironing over the back of the paper. You can buy kits that include several sheets of transfer paper and full instructions on how to print them with any inkjet model.

Similar papers are produced for immortalizing your image on mugs, plates, and a variety of other surfaces, or even to apply to yourself as a temporary tattoo! As you might expect, dozens of online services, not to mention outlets in your local shopping mall, have sprung up to take advantage of this. Photo processing services and the big 'web portals', such as Yahoo!, are good places to try. Surf or shop around, and you'll discover you can get your favourite images reproduced onto mouse mats, bed linen, posters, bibs, baby clothes, and even office stationery items such as notelet holders, pens, and rulers.

Perfect for the last-minute gift!

Gifts Galore!
Remember all those photo-based gifts that your local photo-finisher or minilab used to offer to create from your best negatives? Well, all these and much, much more are available from your digital shots too, and many of them can be ordered online. Jigsaw puzzles, place mats, and coasters are bestsellers, but poster-sized prints are becoming increasingly popular as well.

Unique Gift

Personalise high-q

You can create uniqu
onto our personalise

Mugs

More detai

Engraved Gla
Crystal Gi

More detai

Mugshots

Transferring a photo image to a mug or other piece of china is a great way to use your best photos. You can have these made direct from your digital files via your local photo lab or an online service, or do the job yourself. In either case remember to follow any instructions precisely. You'll find some products are designed to be dishwasher-proof, but others may not be as resilient – so check the maker's descriptions, and be careful with your new family heirlooms!

Digital photos from Digital cameras. Mail order prints and film processing

http://www.bonusprint.co.uk/

Q▾ Google

BONUSPRINT Photo Imaging Professionals

FROM 12p

Digital Photo Printing & Film Processing.

Great Quality Low Cost Photos from your **Film** and **Digital** Cameras by Post.

Get Started   Learn More

Film Processing
From £1.99 !

Personalised
Photo Gifts !

New
Greetings Cards!

99p

Customer
Testimonials:

"Extremely happy..."

From only **£1.99** plus postage (for up to 24 9x13cm photos).
Learn more.

Personalise high-quality gifts with your photos.
Learn more.

One card with a personalised message only 99p! Learn more.

Customer testimonials...

Tell a Friend | Home | Film Processing | Digital Prints | Photo Gifts | Pricing | Help & Support | Links | Legal | Privacy

Rest of the world click here

Photo Gifts – Online digital printing from Bonusprint

http://www.bonusprint.co.uk/pages/photo_gifts.htm?   Q▾ Google

ts with your photos.

birthdays, Christmas or indeed any special occasion by putting your favourite digital photos

Greetings Cards

More details

Mouse Mats

More details

Jewellery

More details

T-Shirts

More details

Jigsaws

More details

Get it on your Chest

Personalized T-shirts featuring your favourite photos or even your own graphics are easy to produce at home in small numbers, or you can order them in larger quantities from a specialist supplier for parties, trips, and so on. And because it's possible to transfer your print to any cotton-based products, you needn't limit yourself to just T-shirts. Kids' clothes or bed linen are possible targets for your work (but make sure you test on a small piece of material to test its willingness to accept the inks).

Glossary (the helpful science bit)

Adobe Inc US company that develops software for specialist, creative tasks such as Web design, graphic design, and video editing. Its products are widely used by both professionals and amateurs. Photoshop, Photoshop Elements, and the video-editing package Premiere are some of its most successful software products.

animated GIF A GIF file containing more than one image. Many programs, including Web browsers, will display each of the images in turn, thus producing an animation.

animation The process of creating a moving image by rapidly moving from one still image to the next. Animations are now commonly created by means of specialist software that renders sequences in a variety of formats, typically QuickTime, AVI, and animated GIF.

antialias/antialiasing The technique of optically eliminating the jagged effect of bitmapped images or text reproduced on low-resolution devices such as monitors.

Apple Computer US-based computer company whose Apple Macintosh computer ('the Mac') was at the forefront of the computing revolution in the 1980s. Its iMac range of computers has revived the company's fortunes in recent years, and its products are still the computers of choice in industries such as publishing, media and advertising (which use them mainly for design-led work). A Mac, though broadly similar, is not the same as a Windows PC, so software designed *solely* for one type of machine will not run successfully on the other. Many popular software packages are available for both platforms, however. Ask your retailer.

attribute The specification applied to a character, box, or other item in a design, layout or image-editing application. Character attributes include font, size, style, colour, shade, scaling, kerning, and so on.

authoring tool/application/ program Software that creates text, drawing, painting, animation, and audio features, and combines these with a scripting language that determines how each element of a page behaves when published on the Internet.

bevel In image-editing software, a chamfered edge that can be applied to type, buttons, or selections to emphasize a three-dimensional effect.

bitmap An array of values specifying the colour of every pixel in a digital image.

bitmapped font One in which the characters are made up of dots, or pixels, as distinct from an outline font, which is drawn from vectors. Bitmapped fonts generally accompany PostScript Type 1 fonts and are used to render the fonts' shapes onscreen.

bitmapped graphic An image made up of dots, or pixels, and usually produced by painting or image-editing applications (as distinct from the vector images of 'object-oriented' drawing applications).

body One of the main structures of an HTML document, falling between the header and the footer.

brightness The strength of luminescence from light to dark.

browser/Web browser Program that enables the viewing or 'browsing' of World Wide Web pages across the Internet. The most commonly used browsers are Netscape's Navigator and Microsoft's Internet Explorer. Version numbers are important, as these indicate the level of HTML that the browser supports. Another browser, 'Opera', is competitive because of its compact size, efficient performance, and security. It is rapidly gaining popularity.

burn(ing) The act of recording data onto a CD in a CD burner (recorder). Software such as Roxio's Toast (Mac) is used for this task when recording from a computer to an external device.

CD-ROM CD (Compact Disc) Read-Only Memory. An evolution of the CD allowing the storage of up to 600 Megabytes of data, such as images, video clips, text and other digital files. But the discs are 'Read only', which means the user can't edit or overwrite the data.

CD-R/CD-RW CD Recordable/ CD-ReWriteable. CD-Rs are inexpensive discs on which you can store any digital data, or roughly 77 minutes of audio (on a hi-fi CD recorder). But once written and finalized (fixed), the data cannot be erased, edited or modified. Similar to the above, CD-RW discs can be 'unfinalized' then overwritten, in part or entirety, any number of times. However, CD-RWs will not play on every type of device – a CD-RW recorded on a hi-fi type of CD recorder will not play on most other CD players.

clip-art/clip media Collections of (usually) royalty-free photographs, illustrations, design devices, and other pre-created items, such as movies, sounds, and 3D wireframes.

clone/cloning In most image-editing packages, Clone tools allow the user to sample pixels (picture elements) from one part of an image, such as a digital photograph, and use them to 'paint' over other areas of the image. The process is useful for removing unwanted parts of an image, or correcting problems, such as closed eyes if the subject blinked while being photographed. In Photoshop and Photoshop Elements, the tool is known as the Rubber Stamp.

colour picker The term describing a colour model when displayed on a computer monitor. Colour pickers may be specific to an application such as Adobe Photoshop, a third-party colour model such as PANTONE, or to the operating system running on your computer.

Composer A simple web page-building package that comes with the Netscape browser.

compression The technique of rearranging data so that it either occupies less space on disk, or transfers faster between devices or over communication lines. For example, high-quality digital images, such as photographs, can take up an enormous amount of disk space, transfer slowly, and use a lot of processing power. They need to be compressed (the file size needs to be made smaller) before they can be published on the Web, as otherwise they would take too long to appear onscreen.

But compressing them can lead to a loss of quality. Compression methods that do not lose data are referred to as 'lossless', while 'lossy' describes methods in which some data is lost.

contrast The degree of difference between adjacent tones in an image from the lightest to the darkest. 'High contrast' describes an image with light highlights and dark shadows, but with few shades in between; while a 'low contrast' image is one with even tones and few dark areas or highlights. These settings are usually editable.

copyright The right of a person who creates an original work to protect that work by controlling how and where it may be reproduced.

copyright-free A misnomer used to describe ready-made resources, such as clip-art. In fact, these resources are rarely, if ever, 'copyright free'. Generally it is only the licence to use the material which is granted by purchase. 'Royalty free' is a more accurate description.

digitize To convert anything, for example, text, images, or sound, into binary form so that it can be digitally processed. In other words, transforming analog data into digital data.

dingbat The modern name for fonts of decorative symbols,

traditionally called printer's 'ornaments', or 'arabesques'.

domain name system/service (DNS) The description of a website's 'address' – the means by which you find or identify a particular website, much like a brand name or trademark. A website address is actually a number that conforms to the numerical Internet protocol (IP) addresses that computers use for information exchange, but names are far easier for us to remember. Domain names are administered by the InterNIC organization and include at least two parts: the 'subdomain', typically a company or organization; and the 'high-level domain', which is the part after the first dot, such as in '.com' for commercial sites, '.org' for non-profit sites, '.gov' for governmental sites, '.edu' for educational sites, and so on.

dots per inch (dpi) A unit of measurement used to represent the resolution of devices such as printers and imagesetters and also, erroneously, monitors and images, whose resolution should more properly be expressed in pixels per inch (ppi). The closer the dots or pixels (the more there are to each inch) the better the quality. Typical resolutions are 72 ppi for a monitor, 600 dpi for a laser printer, and 2,450 dpi (or more) for an imagesetter.

download To transfer data from a remote computer, such as an Internet server, to your own. The opposite of upload.

Dreamweaver Advanced website design software, made by Macromedia, and regarded as the industry standard.

drop shadow A shadow projected onto the background behind an image or character, designed to 'lift' the image or character off the surface.

DVD (Digital Video or Versatile Disk) Similar to CDs and CD-ROMs, DVDs have a storage capacity of up to 18 Gigabytes, far higher than CD-ROMs (600 Megabytes), and can deliver data at a higher rate. This allows DVDs to store up to 10 hours of high-quality MPEG-2 video, and more than 30 hours of medium-quality (more highly compressed) MPEG-1 video footage. DVD drives (players) are becoming standard on many new PCs, and DVD writers will become far less expensive in the near future.

dynamic HTML/DHTML (Dynamic HyperText Markup Language) A development of HTML that enables users to add enhanced features such as basic animations and highlighted buttons to web pages without having to rely on browser plugins.

export A feature provided by many applications to allow you to save a file in a format so that it can be used by another application or on a different operating system. For example, an illustration created in a drawing application may be exported as an EPS file so that it can be used in a page-layout application.

extract A tool and a process in many image-editing applications, such as Photoshop Elements, which allows the selection of part of an image (using the selection tools) and the removal of areas around it, so the subject is extracted from the picture.

eyedropper tool In some applications, a tool for gauging the colour of adjacent pixels.

face Traditionally the printing surface of any metal type character, but nowadays used as a series or family name for fonts with similar characteristics, such as 'modern face'.

file extension The term describing the abbreviated suffix at the end of a filename that describes either its type (such as .eps or .jpg) or origin (the application that created it, such as .qxp for QuarkXPress files).

file format The way a program arranges data so that it can be stored or displayed on a computer. Common file formats are TIFF and JPEG for bitmapped image files, EPS for object-oriented image files and ASCII for text files.

File Transfer Protocol (FTP) A standard system for transmitting files between computers, across the Internet, or over a network. Although most Web browsers incorporate FTP capabilities, dedicated FTP applications offer greater flexibility. Typically, when creating a webpage, an FTP application will be used to 'upload' (send) this to the Web so other people can look at it.

Flash A technology and a software package developed by Macromedia for creating simple and highly complex animations on web pages.

frame (1) A way of breaking up a scrollable browser window on a webpage into several independent windows.

frame (2) A single still picture from a movie or animation sequence. Also a single complete image from a TV picture.

FrontPage Express A cutdown version of Microsoft's web page-building software, which was bundled free with some versions of the Internet Explorer browser.

font Set of characters sharing the same typeface and size.

font file The file of a bitmapped or screen font, usually residing in a suitcase file on Mac computers.

form A special type of web page which provides users with the means to input information directly into the website. Form pages are often used to collect information about visitors, or as a way of collecting password and username data before allowing access to secure areas.

GIF (Graphics Interchange Format) One of the main bitmapped image formats used on the Internet. GIF is a 256-colour format with two specifications, GIF87a and, more recently, GIF89a, the latter providing additional features such as the use of transparent backgrounds. The GIF format uses a 'lossless' compression technique, or 'algorithm', and thus does not squeeze files as much as the JPEG format, which is 'lossy'. For use in Web browsers JPEG is the format of choice for tone images, such as photographs, while GIF is more suitable for line images and other graphics.

graduation/gradation/ gradient The smooth transition from one colour/tone to another. The relationship of reproduced lightness values to original ones in an imaging process, usually expressed as a tone curve.

home page The main, introductory page on a website, usually with a title and tools to navigate through the rest of the site. Also known as the index page or doorway.

host A networked computer that provides services to anyone who can access it, such as for email, file transfer, and access to the Web. When you connect to the Internet, and select a website, information will be transferred to you from the host's computer. Users' computers that request services from a host are often referred to as 'clients'.

HSL (Hue, Saturation, Lightness) A colour model based upon the light transmitted either in an image or in your monitor – hue being the spectral colour (the actual pigment colour), saturation being the intensity of the colour pigment (without black or white added), and brightness representing the strength of luminance from light to dark (the amount of black or white present). Variously called HLS (hue, lightness, saturation), HSV (hue, saturation, value), and HSB (hue, saturation, brightness).

hue A colour found in its pure state in the spectrum.

HTML (HyperText Markup Language) The code that websites are built from. HTML is not a programming language as such, but a set of 'tags' that specify type styles and sizes, the location of graphics, and other information required to construct a web page. To provide for increasingly complex presentations such as animation, sound, and video, the basic form of HTML is seeded with miniature computer programs, or applets.

HTML table A grid on a web page consisting of rows and columns of cells allowing precise positioning of text, pictures, movie clips, or any other element. A table can be nested within another table. Tables offer a way of giving the appearance of multi-column layouts. They can be visible, with cells framed by borders, or invisible and used only to demarcate areas containing the elements on the page. A table is specified in terms of either a pixel count, which fixes its size irrespective of the browser or screen resolution used to view it, or as a percentage of the available screen space, allowing resizing to fit the browser window.

Hypertext Transfer Protocol (http) A text-based set of rules by which files on the World Wide Web are transferred, defining the commands that Web browsers use to communicate with Web servers.

The vast majority of World Wide Web addresses, or 'URLs', are prefixed with 'http://'.

icon A onscreen graphical representation of an object (such as a disk, file, folder, or tool) or a concept, used to make identification and selection easier.

image map An image that features a set of embedded links to other documents or websites. These are activated when the mouse is clicked on the appropriate area. Often the 'front page' of a website contains such a map.

image slicing The practice of dividing up a digital image into rectangular areas or slices, which can then be optimized or animated independently for efficient Web presentation. Programs that enable you to slice images automatically generate an HTML code that puts the slices back together on a web page.

index page The first page of any website that is selected by the browser if it is named 'default.htm', 'default.html', 'index.htm', or 'index.html'.

interactive Any activity that involves an immediate and reciprocal action between a person and a machine (for example, driving a car), but more commonly describing dialog between a computer and its user.

interface This is a term most often used to describe the screen design that links the user with the computer program or website. The quality of the user interface often determines how well users will be able to navigate their way around the pages within the site.

Internet The worldwide network of computers linked by telephone (or other connections), providing individual and corporate users with access to information, companies, newsgroups, discussion areas, and much more.

ISP (Internet Service Provider) An organization that provides access to the Internet. At its most basic this may be a telephone number for connection, but most ISPs provide email addresses and webspace for new sites.

JPEG, JPG The Joint Photographics Experts Group. An ISO (International Standards Organization) group that defines compression standards for bitmapped colour images. The abbreviated form, pronounced 'jay-peg', gives its name to a 'lossy' (meaning some data may be lost) compressed file format in which the degree of compression from high compression and low quality, to low compression and high quality, can be defined by the user.

kerning The adjustment of spacing between two characters (normally alphanumeric) to improve the overall look of the text.

keyline A line drawing indicating the size and position of an illustration in a layout.

layout A drawing that shows the general appearance of a design, indicating, for example, the position of text and illustrations. The term is also used when preparing a design for reproduction, and to describe the way a page is constructed in desktop publishing programs.

link A pointer, such as a highlighted piece of text in an HTML document or multimedia presentation, or an area on an image map, which takes the user to another location, page, or screen just by clicking on it.

lossless/lossy Refers to the data-losing qualities of different compression methods. 'Lossless' means that no image information is lost; 'lossy' means that some (or much) of the image data is lost in the compression process (but the data will download quicker).

Macromedia A software company specializing in Web design, graphics and animation packages.

Microsoft The world's leading software company, whose Windows software for the IBM-compatible PC is now installed on the vast majority of the world's computers. Its Office package, includes Word (the leading wordprocessing package), Excel (the leading spreadsheet and accounting package), and Powerpoint (the slideshow and presentation package). These are also available for the Mac. Recent versions of Windows include the Internet Explorer browser. Despite its success, the company has been accused by rivals of uncompetitive behaviour by including so many of its software packages with new PCs – a charge Microsoft refutes.

midtones/middletones The range of tonal values in an image anywhere between the darkest and lightest, usually referring to those approximately halfway.

multimedia Any combination of various digital media, such as sound, video, animation, graphics, and text, incorporated into a software product or presentation.

paragraph In an HTML document, a markup tag <P> that is used to define a new paragraph in text.

palette This term refers to a subset of colours that are needed to display a particular image. For instance, a GIF image will have a palette containing a maximum of 256 individual and distinct colours.

pixel (picture element) The smallest component of any digitally generated image, including text, such as a single dot of light on a computer screen. In its simplest form, one pixel corresponds to a single bit: 0 = off, or white, and 1 = on, or black. In colour or greyscale images or monitors, one pixel may correspond to several bits. An 8-bit pixel, for example, can be displayed in any of 256 colours (the total number of different configurations that can be achieved by eight 0s and 1s).

plugin Subsidiary software for a browser or other package that enables it to perform additional functions, e.g., play sound, movies, or video.

raster(ization) Deriving from the Latin word 'rastrum', meaning 'rake', the method of displaying (and creating) images employed by video screens, and thus computer monitors, in which the screen image is made up of a pattern of several hundred parallel lines created by an electron beam "raking" the screen from top to bottom at a speed of about one–sixtieth of a second. An image is created by varying the intensity of the beam at successive points along the raster. The speed at which a complete screen image, or frame, is created is called the 'frame' or 'refresh' rate.

rasterize(d) To rasterize is to electronically convert a vector graphics image into a bitmapped image. This may introduce aliasing, but is often necessary when preparing images for the Web; without a plug-in, browsers can only display GIF, JPEG, and PNG image files.

resolution The degree of quality, definition, or clarity with which an image is reproduced or displayed, for example in a photograph, or via a scanner, monitor screen, printer, or other output device.

resolution (2): monitor resolution, screen resolution The number of pixels across by pixels down. The three most common resolutions are 640 x 480, 800 x 600, and 1,024 x 768. The current standard Web page size is 800 x 600.

RGB (Red, Green, Blue) The primary colours of the 'additive' colour model, used in video technology, computer monitors, and for graphics such as for the Web and multimedia that will not ultimately be printed by the four-colour (CMYK) process. CMYK stands for 'Cyan, Magenta, Yellow, BlacK'.

rollover The rapid substitution of one or more images when the mouse pointer is rolled over the original image. Used extensively for navigation buttons on webpages and multimedia presentations.

rollover button A graphic button type that changes in appearance when the mouse pointer moves over it.

scanner An electronic device that converts photographic prints, objects or printed text into digital files by reading them with a beam of light.

scan(ning) An electronic process that converts a hard copy of an image into digital form by sequential exposure to a moving light beam, such as a laser. The scanned image can then be manipulated by a computer or output to separated film.

shareware Software available through user groups, magazine cover disks, etc. Although shareware is not 'copy protected', it is protected by copyright and a fee is normally payable for using it, unlike 'freeware'.

software Computer programs that you can buy, then install into your computer (usually via CD or the Internet), that enable your computer to perform specific tasks, such as photo editing, graphic design, and video-editing. Most recent Windows PC and Apple Mac machines (such as the iMac) come with numerous basic software packages already installed. Free software (known as 'freeware' or, in some circumstances, 'shareware') is also available over the Internet, or on the free CDs that come with many magazines. Software is frequently 'upgraded' by the manufacturer, adding new levels of functionality. Keep your eyes and ears open!

text path In many graphic design, page layout and design software packages, an invisible line – straight, curved, or irregular – along which text can be forced to flow.

thumbnail A small representation of an image used mainly for identification purposes in an image directory listing or, within Photoshop, for illustrating channels and layers. Thumbnails are also produced to accompany PictureCDs, PhotoCDs and most APS and 35mm films submitted for processing.

TIFF, TIF (Tagged Image File Format) A standard and popular graphics file format originally developed by Aldus (now merged with Adobe) and Microsoft, used for scanned, high-resolution, bitmapped images and for colour separations. The TIFF format can be used for black-and-white, greyscale, and colour images, which have been generated on different computer platforms.

tile, tiling Repeating a graphic item and placing the repetitions side-by-side in all directions so that they form a pattern.

transparency Allows a GIF image to be blended into the background by ridding it of unwanted background colour.

tween(ing) A contraction of 'in-between'. An animator's term for the process of creating transitional frames to fill in-between key frames in an animation.

typeface The term (based on 'face' – the printing surface of a metal type character) describing a type design of any size, including weight variations on that design such as light and bold, but excluding all other related designs such as italic and condensed. As distinct from 'type family', which includes all related designs, and 'font', which is one design of a single size, weight, and style. Thus 'Baskerville' is a type family, while 'Baskerville Bold' is a typeface and '9 pt Baskerville Bold Italic' is a font. (But if you use either 'font' or 'typeface' to describe any of the above, no-one will mind!)

Uniform Resource Locator (URL) The unique address of every webpage on the WWW. Every resource on the Internet has a unique URL which begins

with letters that identify the resource type, such as 'http' or 'ftp' (determining the communication protocol to be used), followed by a colon and two forward slashes.

vector A mathematical description of a line that is defined in terms of physical dimensions and direction. Vectors are used in drawing packages (and Photoshop 6 upwards) to define shapes (vector graphics) that are position- and size-independent.

vector graphics Images made up of mathematically defined shapes, such as circles and rectangles, or complex paths built out of mathematically defined curves. Vector graphics images can be displayed at any size or resolution without loss of quality, and are easy to edit because the shapes retain their identity, but they lack the tonal subtlety of bitmapped images. Because vector graphics files are typically small, they are well suited to Web animation.

web page A published HTML document on the World Wide Web, which when linked with others, forms a website, along with other files, such as graphics.

Web server A computer ('host') that is dedicated to Web services.

website The address, location (on a server), and collection of

documents and resources for any particular interlinked set of web pages.

Word The world's leading wordprocessing package, developed by Microsoft for the PC and the Mac. Although designed for creating letters and documents, Word includes simple web page-building functions within its 'Save as HTML' function, found under the 'File' menu.

World Wide Web (WWW) The term used to describe the entire collection of Web servers all over the world that are connected to the Internet. The term also describes the particular type of Internet access architecture that uses a combination of HTML and various graphic formats, such as GIF and JPEG, to publish formatted text that can be read by Web browsers. Colloquially termed simply 'the Web' or, rarely, by the shorthand 'W3'.

World Wide Web Consortium (W3C) The global organization that is largely responsible or maintaining and managing standards across the Web. It is chaired by the UK's Tim Berners Lee, progenitor of the Web.

BOOKS: DIGITAL PHOTOGRAPHY

Perfect Digital Photos in a Snap
Ian Probert and Peter Cope
Ilex Press
ISBN 1-904705-19-7

The Complete Guide to Digital Photography
Michael Freeman
Silver Pixel Press
ISBN 1-883403-91-X

40 Digital Photography Techniques for Beginners
Youngjin.com
Sybex International
ISBN 8-931-43501-0

Bad Pics Fixed Quick: How to Fix Lousy Digital Pictures
Michael Miller
Que
ISBN 0-78973-209-2

The Digital Video Manual
Kyle MacRae
Haynes
ISBN 1-84425-126-8

BOOKS: SOFTWARE

Adobe Photoshop CS for Photographers
Martin Evening
Focal Press
0-24051-942-6

Adobe Photoshop CS in a Book
Adobe Creative Team
Adobe Press
0-32119-375-X

Adobe Photoshop CS One-on-One
Deke McClelland
O'Reilly & Associates
0-59600-618-7

Adobe Photoshop CS Down & Dirty Tricks
Scott Kelby
New Riders Press
0-73571-353-7

How to do Everything with Paint Shop Pro 8
David Huss
McGraw-Hill Osborne Media
0-07219-107-4

Paint Shop Pro 8 for Dummies
David C. Kay, William Steinmetz
For Dummies
0-76452-440-2

WEBSITES: DIGITAL IMAGING, PHOTOGRAPHY

Note that website addresses can change, and sites can appear and disappear almost daily. Use a search engine to help you find new arrivals or check addresses.

The Complete Guide to Digital Photography
www.completeguidctodigitalphotography.com

Creativepro
("news and resources for creative professionals")
www.creativepro.com

The Digital Camera Resource Page
(consumer-oriented resource)
www.dcresource.com

Digital Photography
(news and reviews)
www.digital-photography.org

Digital Photography Review
www.dpreview.com

ePHOTOzine
www.ephotozine.com

The Imaging Resource
(news and reviews)
www.imaging-resource.com

Photolink International
(education in photography and related fields)
www.photoeducation.net

photo.net
(photography resource site: community, advice, gallery, tutorials)
www.photo.net

ShortCourses: Digital Photography: Theory and Practice
www.shortcourses.com

WEBSITES: SOFTWARE

Paintshop Pro
www.jasc.com

PhotoImpact, PhotoExpress
www.ulead.com

Photo-Paint, CorelDRAW!
www.corel.com

Photoshop, Photoshop Elements, ImageReady, Illustrator
www.adobe.com

Photosuite
www.mgisoft.com

Picture Publisher
www.micrografx.com